Winning the unfair fight

Winning the unfair fight

HOW YOUR SMALL BUSINESS CAN TAKE ON, AND BEAT, THE GIANTS

★ ★ ★ ★ ★

SAM HAZLEDINE

Published by Penguin Books (South Africa) (Pty) Ltd, 2015
This edition by Portfolio Penguin, an imprint of Penguin Books,
a Penguin Random House company

Registered offices: Block D, Rosebank Office Park, 181 Jan Smuts Avenue,
Parktown North, Johannesburg 2193, South Africa

www.penguinbooks.co.za

First published by Random House New Zealand in 2014
This edition © Portfolio Penguin, 2015

1 3 5 7 9 10 8 6 4 2

Copyright © Sam Hazledine, 2015

ISBN 978 1 77022 826 9

PUBLISHER: Marlene Fryer
EDITOR: Ronel Richter-Herbert
PROOFREADER: Bronwen Leak
COVER DESIGN: Sean Robertson
TEXT DESIGN: Monique Cleghorn
TYPESETTER: Monique van den Berg

Set in 12 pt on 16.5 pt Janson MT

Printed and bound by Replika Press Pvt Ltd, India

CONTENTS

This book is dedicated to the three most important people in my life: Claire, Zara and Florence. I said I wouldn't dedicate a book to you until I wrote one that was worthy. This is it.

THIS BOOK IS FOR …

… every small- to medium-sized business owner who knows they could be more successful, who realises there is more.

… every business owner who's struggling and exhausted. I know you are working incredibly hard, but sometimes it can be so difficult to know what step to take next. I know the playing field doesn't seem fair, but you can turn the tables in your favour.

I've written this book because I've been in your situation. I understand just how hard it is, and I've found a way to make it much easier.

It's still going to take hard work, but I know you are no stranger to that. I am excited to know that you are taking the first step today towards creating a really successful business, because that is going to have a huge impact on you, your family, your employees, your customers and your country.

Today is the day to put struggle behind you and to create the business you envisaged when you first started.

ACKNOWLEDGEMENTS

I have been incredibly fortunate to have had many great teachers in my life. This book has been hugely influenced by the works of these people – thank you for the impact each of you have had.

To my wife Claire, thank you for teaching me by example how to be a kinder person, and for giving me the most important reason to be that person.

To my daughters Zara and Florence, thank you for teaching me to be present and to cherish every moment of life.

To Mom and Dad, thank you for instilling in me the belief that anything is possible, because this has shaped my entire life.

To Keith Cunningham, thank you for teaching me how to move beyond flash-in-the-pan 'wins' to creating sustainable business success; your influence is found throughout this book, and in my everyday business practice.

To Anthony Robbins, thank you for teaching me that success starts with a powerful personal psychology and for teaching me tools to improve mine; your influence is also found throughout this book.

To Deb Battersby, thank you for being my 'secret weapon' and for helping me to move through my own blocks to success.

To Richard Petrie, thank you for teaching me the importance of getting my message across to the people who need to hear it.

To Garry Kewish, thank you for teaching me the importance of having a sales system.

To the Brotherhood, thank you for being an incredible peer group, and inspiring me to achieve great things.

To my board, thank you for holding me accountable and for calling it tight.

To my team at MedRecruit, thank you for teaching me the importance of 'A-players' in achieving business success, and the fact that there are a lot of people much better suited to many aspects of business than me; it's a privilege to be on the journey with you.

And to you, the reader, thank you for believing in me and for reading this book. I appreciate you and I hold your trust in the highest regard. I won't let you down.

SAM HAZLEDINE

INTRODUCTION

Compete Head to Head and You're Dead

Small businesses are the backbone of the economy, with 97 per cent of businesses having 19 or fewer staff, and 87 per cent employing fewer than five staff. But most small business owners are trying to compete head to head against corporate Goliaths, and subsequently up to 96 per cent ultimately fail.

Business isn't paintball; your competition is playing with live rounds. If you get shot, you don't get to sit out for five minutes and then rejoin the game – you're dead.

If you're fighting fair, then you have failed to prepare.

A fair fight means you're playing on their terms and it's anyone's game. If you're not using all the unique resources available to you to gain an advantage, then you are taking a massive gamble, and you will likely join the majority of business owners who go broke.

There's a place for fighting fair, for rolling the dice, and that's when you don't care whether you win or lose – that's the place for hobbies. But if you need to win, if your life, your business, your future depends on it, then don't gamble.

If you want to ensure that your own business succeeds, you need to learn the art of the Unfair Fight, where you act with total integrity –

not playing dirty, but playing by your own rules, where you think and act in ways that drive success, and you move beyond the fight to a place where you have transcended the competition.

WHAT IS THE UNFAIR FIGHT?

The year was 1000 BC. The Philistines had gathered for war against Israel, the two armies facing each other on opposite sides of the Valley of Elah. Each day for 40 days, the Philistines sent out one of their men, a giant over nine feet tall, to mock and challenge the Israelites. His name was Goliath.

Saul, the King of Israel, and his whole army were terrified of Goliath.

One day David, a young shepherd, was sent to the battle lines by his father to bring back news of his brothers. While there, David heard Goliath shouting his daily defiance, and he responded, 'Who is this uncircumcised Philistine that he should defy the armies of God?'

David wouldn't lay down and be beaten by the bully, so he volunteered to fight Goliath. King Saul wasn't convinced at first. Why did this young man, who had nowhere near the battle experience or stature of Goliath, have the confidence to take on this giant? The king finally agreed, knowing that David, while seemingly outmatched, was their only hope of winning. David approached Goliath dressed in a simple tunic and carrying just a slingshot and a pouch full of stones.

David said to the Philistine, 'You come against me with sword and spear and javelin, but I come against you in the name of the Lord Almighty, and today I will feed your carcass to the birds.'

David knew he had an unfair advantage. But no one else could see it.

As Goliath moved closer, David reached into his bag, took out a stone, placed it in his slingshot and aimed the stone at Goliath's head. The stone sank into the giant's forehead and he fell to the ground.

David grabbed Goliath's sword and killed him, and then cut off his head. When the Philistines saw that their hero was dead, they turned and ran.

This is the Unfair Fight.

THE UNFAIR FIGHT AND YOU

The Unfair Fight is a way of winning the battle in the face of seeming adversity. The Unfair Fight is a way of playing by your own rules. The Unfair Fight is a way of stepping up with absolute confidence and certainty, knowing victory is yours because you have transcended the competition.

In the Unfair Fight there are three winners: your customers, your employees and you.

Your customers win because you cut straight to what's important to them; you communicate with them by entering the conversation that's already going on in their head; you sell to them by providing solutions in a way that they understand and that exceed their needs; you deliver your product or service to them with seamless execution; and you give them the benefit of a single, stable supplier.

Your employees win because you create an environment in which they can be their best; you provide a culture in which they can thrive; and you have a business that can reward them better than your competition.

And *you* win because you make your business stand out from any of the competition as the only logical and emotional choice, and you create long-term sustainable profitability.

WHY IS THE UNFAIR FIGHT NECESSARY?

People generally start businesses with hope, with excitement, with a dream to create something better for themselves, their families, and for their employees and customers. They often enter markets dominated by big corporates, the Goliaths, and they try to compete with them as if it is a level playing field.

But the playing field isn't level. Big companies have much deeper pockets than you. They have more experienced management teams than you. They have infinitely larger marketing budgets than you. And they have a vested interest in seeing you fail so that they can maintain their market dominance.

If you compete head to head with these big companies, and play by their rules, you will lose every time.

But big companies are also less flexible and slower to adapt and innovate.

We all know David would not have beaten Goliath in a battle of strength – Goliath would have crushed him. If you try to compete with the bigger companies in the same way they compete against you, you will be crushed.

David beat Goliath because he out-thought him; he used the resources available to him to create an Unfair Fight. He turned his perceived weaknesses into strengths. He acted with total integrity: he didn't break any laws, he didn't play dirty, but he did play by his own rules and changed the game so that he couldn't lose.

This is the essence of the Unfair Fight.

Why is it absolutely necessary for you to learn and apply the Unfair Fight? Most business books and resources are developed from studying big corporates, so they give you strategies and tactics that are akin to giving you better arm-wrestling techniques for fighting against Arnold Schwarzenegger. If you're arm-wrestling Arnie, it doesn't matter how you grip his hand, what you focus on or how fiercely you stare into his eyes, sending fear deep into his soul … you're going to lose.

Similarly, if you study how the corporates do business and then try to apply those strategies to your own business, you're going to lose, because you don't have all the resources that go with being a massive corporate.

The only way you can win is if you change the game and come at it from a different approach; you don't attack a giant head-on.

If you were to look at all of the wars that have been waged over the past 200 years between completely unmatched sides, where one army was at least 10 times larger than the other, as political scientist Ivan Arreguín-Toft did (also discussed in Malcolm Gladwell's book *David and Goliath*), then you would expect the much larger and more powerful army to win every time. After all, 10 times the size and power is a completely unfair fight, isn't it? However, what he found was that the larger army won only 71.5 per cent of the time – so the small guy didn't always get beaten by the bigger guy.

Arreguín-Toft then looked a little deeper to find out what happens between strong and weak armies when the weak army does as David did and refuses to play by the same rules as the stronger army, using unconventional or guerrilla tactics. And the answer gets really interesting: now the weaker side's chances of being victorious went from 28.5 per cent to 63.6 per cent – they actually gave themselves the advantage.

We think that underdogs are less likely to win, that the odds are not stacked in their favour. But the reality is that the underdog, the smaller business, can utilise strategies and tactics that the big guys, the large corporates, never can.

We assume that the underdog is less likely to win, but when you know how to apply unconventional tactics to your business, you become like David – Goliath could never actually have beaten him, as David was fighting with a tool that the lumbering giant could never counter. David wasn't the underdog – in reality, he was the favourite.

And so are you. You can exploit your advantages – advantages that your bigger competitors don't have – and start being victorious in business.

The time has come for you to stop competing on someone else's terms and start winning on your own terms with the art of the Unfair Fight.

GOOD DAYS AND BAD DAYS

In life you're going to have good days and you're going to have bad days, and what's certain is that at the end of each day you're not always going to know which was which.

On 20 June 2002, after trying to backflip off a two-metre-high wall at a local bar, I sustained a head injury that nearly killed me.

Prior to that day I had been living my life recklessly. I had been living in a way that wasn't good for me, and it certainly wasn't good for other people.

My parents got a call at 2.30 a.m. to say that they should get to Dunedin because the doctors weren't sure that I would ever come out of the coma.

At the time they would have called it a bad day.

When I came out of the coma a few days later, the doctors said that I would probably not regain full brain function, I would be unlikely to return to medical school and I would certainly never ski again.

I definitely thought it was a bad day.

I think lessons come in three forms ...

First, there are 'feather' lessons, those niggles that indicate something's not quite right and a change is needed. I ignored all the 'feathers'.

If you ignore enough 'feathers', then you get 'brick' lessons. This second type of lesson is a lot less subtle and, for most people, it is enough to induce change.

But I ignored the 'bricks', so I got the 'Mack Truck' lesson– the third lesson, which is the lesson that cannot be ignored. It comes along and bowls you over and says, 'Change is a must.'

You don't always survive the Mack Truck lessons.

The head injury was my Mack Truck.

The head injury made me realise that for my life to change, first *I* had to change. I realised that for my life to improve, I had to raise my standards. After the head injury I was in such deep physical, emotional and spiritual pain that I went about raising the standards of my life like a fanatic.

With the support of my family, and with my total commitment to coming back stronger, I returned to medical school within three months; within six months I regained full brain function and met my future wife Claire; and the following year I became the New Zealand extreme ski champion.

I learnt that by raising my standards I could make my life into something I could be proud of, something that was not only good for me, but was also good for others.

It turned out 20 June 2002 was a great day.

The reason I'm sharing this story with you is because you don't need to wait until you get the Mack Truck lesson to change your life. You don't need to roll the dice and wait until you could be killed, either literally or figuratively.

The lesson in raising standards is an important one.

I am sure that one of the reasons you are reading this book is that your business is not where you want it to be right now. Remember this: Your business and the current state it is in is exactly where you *need* it to be. It's a direct reflection of the standards you currently have.

But today is a good day – if you decide to make it that way.

The realisation that your business is where you *need* it to be can be scary when you first comprehend it, but then you will become aware of its brilliance – because the first step is to *need* your business to become better, and by raising your standards you *can* make it better.

DELAYED GRATIFICATION TO CONSISTENT GRATIFICATION

When I first decided to raise my standards I had to stop living in the world of immediate gratification. The way I had been living meant that I took whatever I wanted to feel good in the moment, but I certainly didn't feel good in the long term, and it certainly didn't make others feel good.

With the head injury came so much emotional pain that I forced myself to delay gratification, to focus on what I needed to do to get better. I knew I had very little room for error; one or two wrong moves and I might not recover. I had to do this for so long that delayed gratification became a habit.

But then something funny happened. I started to achieve really great things in my life and to feel really good, seemingly by delaying gratification and moving my life towards what really mattered. I had made the transition from delayed gratification to consistent gratification without realising it.

This transition has meant that I am not only able to succeed, but I'm able to sustain and improve on that success.

I am certainly no Deepak Chopra, so I realised that a process had happened. It took some time to figure out exactly what had taken place, and I'll share it now because I think that all consistently successful people go through this process, whether their success is in business, sport, family or anything else. By understanding this process, and by understanding that as the process develops you start feeling better and you start getting what you want, I think you'll be able to stick with it, and you'll be able to master the lessons of this book.

First, you need to get clear about what you want and what you

need to do to get there. *Winning the Unfair Fight* will give you a clear path to create a successful business.

By getting clear on what you need to do, it will become apparent that there are certain things you need to *stop* doing. Every time we say 'Yes' to something, we are saying 'No' to something else. We do everything for a reason, and that reason is often immediate gratification, to gain pleasure in the moment or to avoid pain in the moment.

Now that you have identified what you need to do, you must do it consistently, and consistently stop doing the things that won't get you where you want to be. In the short term, this delayed gratification might feel uncomfortable, and it might be hard to stick with. But you know now that immediate gratification and delayed gratification are both just habits.

Habits are simply neural pathways, routes in your brain that are easy to travel. The reason you travel on these well-known pathways is because at some level they satisfy your rules about feeling good. Gratification is just a feeling, and feelings are completely created by you. If something makes you feel good, it just means you have allowed yourself to satisfy your rules for feeling good.

By delaying gratification, you are choosing to create a new neural pathway, a new habit. At the start this might feel uncomfortable, because creating a new path through a thick forest is hard work, but the more you walk the path, the clearer the path becomes and the easier it is to walk. Before long, if you remain consistent, you will have created a totally new pathway, and your old pathway will have become overgrown. You have now effectively created a new 'easy' route for your brain to travel, a new route that gets you where you want to be and also makes you feel good.

You have consciously created a new way of thinking that will help move your life forward.

Learning to keep raising my standards and training myself to get pleasure from doing things that bring me closer to what I want are two of the most important lessons that have led to my success.

For me, it took almost losing my life, but it doesn't have to be like that. Anyone can choose to raise their standards. *You* can choose to raise your standards and train yourself to get pleasure from doing what you need to do to move your life forward.

If you have struggled in the past to achieve the results you want in life, or in business, then reflect on this: *It's not complicated and anyone can do it.*

Trust me, if I can do it, then anyone can.

And it makes all the difference.

CREATING BUSINESS SUCCESS IN AN UNFAIR WORLD

When I set up my first business, MedRecruit, I had no business or recruitment experience. I hadn't studied business, and I was entering a market where one company had a total monopoly.

We are a recruitment company that places doctors in hospitals throughout Australia and New Zealand, but at the start we had neither hospitals nor doctors. Not a great position for a recruitment company!

It was an Unfair Fight, and by all accounts I should have failed. I would have if I'd played by the rules of traditional business teaching. But because I was smaller, I needed to be smarter: I learnt that my advantage over the bigger competition lay in being nimble; I learnt that I could study and apply knowledge faster than anyone else; and I learnt that I could develop a success mindset that almost guaranteed results – I developed the art of the Unfair Fight.

The Unfair Fight turns perceived weaknesses into strengths.

Over a six-year period I grew my company to be the market leader. We featured in the Deloitte Fast 50 for four consecutive years, and in 2012 I became the Ernst & Young Young Entrepreneur of the Year.

People constantly ask me if I'm surprised at my level of success and my answer is always no, because I know that the art of the Unfair Fight means I have a massive advantage.

Great entrepreneurs know they are on an unfair playing field, so they focus on today and have a road map for tomorrow. They answer the question 'How can I meet a need right now?' while keeping in mind what the industry is going to look like 10 years from now, and preparing for that change.

Many business owners think business success is complicated; it is not, but it is also not easy. Business success takes a commitment to relentlessly focus on what matters, and that's exactly what this book is about. It shows you *exactly* what you need to focus on so that the deck is stacked in your favour.

BUSINESS SUCCESS LIES AT THE INTERSECTION OF MINDSET AND ACTION

This business book is different from most business books.

Almost all business books focus 100 per cent on what to *do* to be successful in business. Very few business books focus on *how to think* to be successful in business. Almost no business books cover both.

The Pareto Principle states that for many events, roughly 80 per cent of the effects come from 20 per cent of the causes. It is a common rule of thumb in business, but it focuses solely on what you *do* to get the results.

In my experience, the 80:20 rule of business success is that only 20 per cent of your success comes from what you *do*, and a massive 80 per cent of your success comes from how you *think* – your personal psychology.

To be extremely successful in business, you need both parts working exceptionally well together; you need a powerful personal psychology combined with taking the right actions.

Winning the Unfair Fight is unique in that it focuses on both important factors to create business success. In Part 1, it gives you the best of the best personal psychology, and in Part 2, it gives you the best of the best actions to take.

If you are someone who prefers one to the other, actions or mindset, then you are reading the right book, because it's likely that the part you are currently missing is the part you don't embrace to the same extent. Lean into it during this book and lift the lid on what's possible for you and your business.

Your commitment to both is critical to your success, because true success lies at the intersection.

YOU'RE GOING TO HAVE TO DO THE PUSH-UPS

As the late personal-development expert Jim Rohn said, 'You can't hire someone else to do your push-ups for you.' Your success is your responsibility, and if you want to make your business extremely successful, you're going to have to do the push-ups. You need to take 100 per cent responsibility for your results and give up blame, complaining, justification, defensiveness and making excuses.

In business there are many moving parts and it can be challenging to be extremely successful. I think of business as being like ski racing: you have to learn how to turn quickly and powerfully but, every time you race, the course has changed and the gates are in different places. You may be able to make perfect turns, but making the same turn over and over again will mean you might miss the gates and be disqualified.

With the rate of change in the world, and in business, having a three- to five-year business plan locked in is like ski racing, where you expect the gates to stay in the same place every time – it's a joke, because the world will have changed by the time you press 'print' on your perfectly formatted plan. What you need are principles to apply so you can continually adjust your turns to continually adapt to the changing course.

In the words of Keith Cunningham, 'Structure is the price entrepreneurs have to pay for success', to make the fight unfair *in your favour*. This book gives you a proven structure to succeed, and within this structure it allows you to be creative, as essentially business is both an art and a science.

If you have the combination to a lock, then you can open it; it doesn't matter if you're young or old, fat or thin, rich or poor, or have an IQ of 150 or an IQ of 90. If you have the combination, the lock will open.

Winning the Unfair Fight is the combination to unlocking your business success, the right balance between how to think and what to do.

Business is the most exciting and rewarding career I know of, and it's a lot more fun when you're doing well. I love the thrill of creating something awesome, of showing people what's possible, of delivering incredible results to customers, of enriching the lives of my staff, and of being in control of my own destiny. And as if that's not enough of a reward, making a truckload of money is pretty cool, too.

> *'We are all self-made, but only the successful will admit it.'*
> — EARL NIGHTINGALE

Most people won't even finish this book; in my experience, 90 per cent never finish a book they pick up. Of those who do finish, another 90 per cent won't do anything with it; the 1 per cent who read the book and apply its strategies will get all the rewards. That 1 per cent chooses to raise their standards and train themselves to enjoy what is good for them. This is the essence of the Unfair Fight – having the right strategy and doing what unsuccessful people aren't prepared to do. So, when people ask if you're surprised at your success, you will be able to say, like I do, that it was inevitable.

I wasn't a business genius when I started my first company. I was just hungrier for success than most, so I learnt more and applied things faster than anyone else. If I'd had a book like this, I could have taken years off my growth curve. The fact that 96 per cent of businesses ultimately fail is no coincidence when you consider how many business owners will read this AND take action.

You are self-made. Don't do yourself the disservice of pretending otherwise. You choose what self that is; whether you are incredibly successful, or mediocre, you are self-made.

My vision is that you will be the minority who makes the decision to succeed.

My vision is that you will be proud to say 'I am self-made', not embarrassed.

Welcome to a new way of doing business.

Welcome to the Unfair Fight.

WHAT IS THE UNFAIR FIGHT WORTH TO YOU?

In the United States, the average person with a bachelor's degree earns about US$2.1 million in their entire lifetime. If you get yourself a master's degree, you can raise that to US$2.5 million, or make that a doctorate and you're up to US$3.4 million.

If you just finish high school, then you're on track to earn less than US$1.2 million in your entire lifetime!

That's all.

I know from personal experience that when you are successful in business, you can make more than this every year. In fact, according to the bestselling author Brian Tracy, 74 per cent of self-made millionaires create their wealth from starting businesses and building them from the ground up.

With a successful business you can literally start with nothing and become incredibly wealthy.

I am not telling you this to impress you, but to impress upon you that this information is valuable.

The Unfair Fight is the blueprint for achieving these results.

I believe anyone can master the Unfair Fight and become someone who creates incredibly profitable businesses – clearing one million a year will become your baseline, not your target.

By doing this, you can raise your lifetime earnings to well in excess of $40 million.

Learning and applying the Unfair Fight is the best investment you can make in your future. The difference to your life will be astronomical.

What difference would making $40 million in your lifetime mean for your life and the lives of the people you care about, compared to lifetime earnings of $2 million?

How much bigger an impact could you have in the world with that level of income?

And going beyond just the money, how do you feel about yourself when you are living on purpose, doing great things, living your potential?

What's that worth to you?

That's the value of the Unfair Fight.

HOW TO USE THE UNFAIR FIGHT

For the Unfair Fight to be effective, it is important to keep five core strategies at the front of your mind:

1. Do it

This book includes only the best, most effective and most important strategies for your business. No paragraph is here as a filler; every sentence is important.

I recommend that you read the book once, quickly, to get an overall impression of what's possible. Then, if you're serious about creating excellence and the results you want, read through it again carefully and act on every step, taking your time, but not taking *too* much time.

Alternatively, you can complete every exercise and take action on your first read-through.

Entrepreneurship without action is like studying music without listening to it. Take action on what you learn, confront any fears or discomfort head-on, and begin the process of creating an exceptional business.

2. Do it badly

There's an old saying that if something's worth doing, it's worth doing well.

How is that working out for you?

How many things have you procrastinated over, or completely failed to start, because you were too worried about getting it right, about doing it perfectly?

I think this is a better saying: 'If it's worth doing, then it's worth doing badly.'

I don't mean that you should deliberately set out to do something badly, but acknowledge that you are unlikely to get it perfect the first time. Then you will be able to learn from what you did and ultimately do a good job.

3. Fail fast

> *'I've not failed. I've just found 10 000 ways that won't work.'*
> — THOMAS EDISON

The most successful people are the people who have failed the most. They aren't afraid of failure, because they know that every failure is a step closer to success. One powerful belief I have adopted is that if I fail fast and learn from it, then it's not failure at all.

In a year's time, would you rather have tried a dozen marketing initiatives, found the three that worked incredibly well, improved on them and started generating more leads than your business can handle – or would you rather be still perfecting your marketing plan and talking about how great it will be?

4. Persist

> *'Opportunity is missed by most people because*
> *it is dressed in overalls and looks like work.'*
>
> — THOMAS EDISON

This is not a book you can read and then magically manifest everything you ever dreamt of by lying on the couch and visualising it.

It's going to take some effort on your part.

The great thing is that you're getting on the fast track. If you're prepared to work hard, *Winning the Unfair Fight* gives you exactly what you need to grow your business exponentially, to make the competition obsolete and to become as successful as you decide. Make sure you do the exercises in each chapter and implement them in your business.

Give it your best effort and refine as you go – remember, don't worry about getting it perfect.

The simple formula for success is if you fall down 1 000 times, then get up 1 001 times. Don't expect to get everything right the first time, but make sure you get back up if you do trip.

5. Astound yourself

> *'If we did all the things we are capable of,*
> *we would literally astound ourselves.'*
>
> — THOMAS EDISON

When you put into action what you learn in this book, you are going to astound yourself by how successful you can be. Right now you might be struggling in your business, you might be doing okay, or you might be doing very well; regardless, you are not at your full potential. There is so much more you are capable of, and this book will give you many tools to realise that potential.

The difference between potential and success is that potential is still talking about it, while success has done it.

Do it.

Astound yourself.

WHAT STAGE IS YOUR BUSINESS AT?

Doing the Right Thing at the Right Time

In business, as in anything, doing the right thing at the right time is critical.

If you bought property in 2003 and sold it in 2007, then you were a genius; if you bought in 2008 and sold in 2012, then you probably weren't!

Same thing, different time – completely different results.

Everything in life moves through cycles. Just as a person is born, grows, matures, and eventually experiences decline and death, so, too, does an industry and a business.

At every stage, while the questions might remain the same, the answers keep changing.

In business you need to be aware of two life cycles: your industry's life cycle and your business's life cycle.

It is crucial that you understand both life cycles, so that you not only do the right thing, but also do it at the right time.

This chapter will help you determine what stage your business is at, and what stage your industry is at. As a result, you will be able to more effectively prioritise and apply the most appropriate and relevant lessons of the Unfair Fight – at the right time.

The reason this chapter comes before the action steps is because getting clear on the stage you are at will allow you to prioritise what's important more effectively. A map is no good unless you know from where you are starting – this chapter is for you to determine where your business is currently at on the road to success.

THE LIFE CYCLE OF AN INDUSTRY

The first thing for you to do is to work out which of the four stages your industry is at in its life cycle: Introduction, Growth, Maturity or Decline.

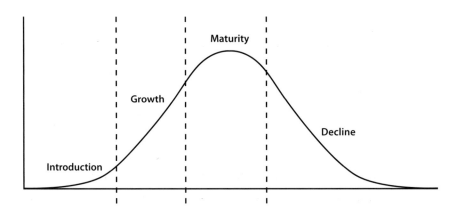

Introduction

This is the very start of an industry; perhaps it's the introduction of a new and unique product. It's an exciting time and a business in this industry might be completely alone.

A company will use the uniqueness of its product or service to attract 'innovators' and 'early adopters' to try it out. Marketing during this stage is intended to explain its uses to potential customers and to create awareness – after all, it is completely new. A company can effectively establish dominance in its niche at this stage. For example, it often aims to build perceptions of superior quality or technological breakthroughs to develop a competitive advantage.

A main focus for a business in this phase is testing the idea to see if it will be viable; it's an expensive exercise and, for this reason, a business at this stage is rarely profitable. Its objective is to validate the idea while spending the least possible amount of money. In Silicon Valley, they call this MVP – minimum viable product. The idea is to minimise the investment until you know there's a market.

An industry often doesn't progress past this stage because there is a high risk of new ideas never being adopted by the market.

You know your industry is at Introduction if you are pioneers with little or no direct competition.

STRATEGY FOR SUCCESS
Innovation and validating the idea

Growth

In the Growth phase, the idea has been validated and other competitors are joining the market. Marketing is aimed at differentiating a business's offering compared to its competitors'.

A high-growth industry with an ever-expanding pie can be a bit like the Wild West – there's enough for everyone and businesses go about grabbing as much as they possibly can, while the pie continues to expand.

However, the customers are the 'early and middle majorities' whose standards for quality are higher, so businesses place a significant focus on product standardisation, on creating consistent quality, which may encourage economies of scale.

Investment goes into evolving the product or service to better meet the needs and wants of the customers. If a business is successful at this stage, the growing demand will drive sales. Customers become your greatest advocates and word of mouth is vital.

Later in this phase, as the product or service becomes more widely accepted, new businesses enter the market and competition increases.

Growth in much of this phase is fast and businesses tend to spread geographically to make the most of the trend.

You know your industry is in Growth if there are a number of successful businesses growing quickly in a market whose size also keeps growing.

STRATEGY FOR SUCCESS
Development, differentiation and expansion

Maturity

As more competition from late entrants floods the industry, the marketing efforts of each business must continue to stress the unique benefits and features of its product or service and continue to differentiate itself from the competitors.

At this stage, businesses can choose to differentiate on quality or on price. As industries continue to mature, there are fewer and fewer players as a smaller number take market share and innovation slows.

This stage can continue for many years.

New entrants must have a significant competitive advantage in their business model to enter a mature industry and succeed.

You know your industry is in Maturity if the market growth is slowing or is flat, and if market leaders are emerging and gaining dominance.

Decline

Decline is almost inevitable because innovation outside an industry invariably causes that industry to become obsolete. For instance, after the advent of the compact disc, the days were numbered for producers of vinyl records, no matter how good the operators were. And the same has now happened for the compact disc as music has moved online. It's a never-ending process driven by continual innovation.

As a result sales suffer, large companies exit the industry and fewer companies remain to compete in the smaller market. Growth usually comes through merger-and-acquisition activity.

It's important for companies in industries at this stage to focus on the segments of their market that are growing, and to look at diversification beyond their specific industry to other industries where they can gain leverage.

You know your industry is in Decline if the big players are leaving and smaller players are scrambling to pick up the scraps.

STRATEGY FOR SUCCESS

Innovative uses for product and diversification

Knowing what stage your industry is at is critical so that you can focus your energy on the most appropriate and effective strategies for success.

THE LIFE CYCLE OF A BUSINESS

As well as having a clear understanding of the life cycle of your industry, it's important to have an understanding of what stage your own business is at in its own life cycle. This is because the requirements, opportunities, challenges and threats that are present will vary with your business's stage of development; what's appropriate and normal at each stage is quite different, and how you move to the next stage requires different actions. Understanding both where you are and where you are going gives you an insight into the road ahead and allows you to act in the right way.

It's important to note that a business's life cyle operates independently of the industry life cycle.

Some problems, in life and in business, are both normal and desirable; they are the result of change. As a business owner, your job is not to prevent problems but to accelerate your organisation's ability to recognise and resolve them, and to create higher-quality problems. Many normal problems don't require your attention because they will resolve themselves in the usual course of your development. On the other hand, some problems are abnormal. Because you will have so much going on, you need to recognise which are abnormal for the stage you are at and solve those difficulties.

Focus your limited time and resources where they are most needed to get the biggest return.

The authority on this work is management expert Dr Ichak Adizes, and much of this section is adapted from his book *Managing Corporate Lifecycles*, which Dr Adizes has kindly granted me permission to use. While the stages have different names, and some of the content is also different and related to my own experience, it was in *Managing Corporate Lifecycles* that I was introduced to the concept of life cycles of businesses.

As businesses make their transition through the different stages, the balance between flexibility and control is constantly tested, as are the two forces of external and internal focus. This 'dance' is what trips up many business owners, because the right thing at one stage may be the kiss of death at another.

As you read this section, try to identify which of the seven stages your business is at. While you might recognise traits in more than one stage, the likelihood is that there will be one that resonates most powerfully.

'Normal problems' are to be expected at all stages; be aware of these, but don't get too worried about them.

'Abnormal problems' are the difficulties that need your attention and must be solved, because they can spell the demise of your business.

'Pathologies' are life-threatening problems that must be addressed swiftly. These are not 'to be expected', and without immediate life support a business with these problems won't survive.

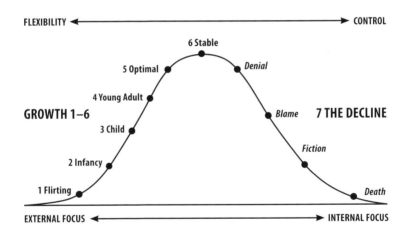

Stage 1: Flirting

Flirting is the first stage of an organisation's development, when it is just a twinkle in the founder's eye. The focus is on dreams and possibilities, and the primary goal is to build the founder's enthusiasm and commitment to their dream; the higher the risk, the deeper the necessary commitment, because the more you're going to have to lay on the line.

As Conrad Hilton said, 'If you want to launch big ships, you have to go where the water is deep.'

Normal problems
- Overexcitement
- Unclear on the details
- Fear and doubt

Abnormal problems
- Low commitment
- Apathy
- Paralysis through analysis – stalling
- Arrogance
- Exclusive focus on making money

Pathologies
- Lack of passion and enthusiasm
- Quitting at the first sign of difficulty

Action required
Decide. If you don't have passion and enthusiasm now, don't expect to get it later. Either get it or quit before you waste time and money. Cut out all other options and decide to move your idea forward. This is a critical step that is covered in depth in Round 1 of the Unfair Fight (see page 47).

Moving on
Financially commit to creating the business.

Stage 2: Infancy

'It's a … business!'

Infancy begins when financial risk has been undertaken; the business is no longer just being talked about, it's really happening. Infant organisations are action-orientated and opportunity driven, and the focus constantly changes from coming up with ideas to taking action to produce results.

Like a baby, Infant organisations need two things:
1. Nourishment in the form of money.
2. Unconditional love from the founder.

Infant organisations lack systems, and this makes delegation difficult. While many business books talk about the importance of delegation, now is not the time for it, because being involved in everything is the only way the founder can maintain some control.

Parents can't delegate nappy changing and feeding because they only want to do the fun stuff like playing; they have to be all-in. You can't just buy a manual, give it to a nanny and say, 'See you in 18 years when you've raised my child!'

And while Infant organisations chase sales because they need the cash, the biggest benefit of sales is market validation of the business's idea – this stage answers the question: 'Do I have a viable business?'

Normal problems
- Erratic performance
- Lack of systems
- Chasing sales
- Changing product or service
- Management from crisis to crisis
- Total reliance on the founder

- Stress on family and home life
- Negative cash flow

Abnormal problems
- Rushing the product or service to market before it is ready
- Trying to perfect products or services without market validation
- Unable to close key sales
- Unable to respond to product failure
- Rigid rules and procedures
- No tolerance for error
- Leaders out of touch
- Control spread across too many people – too much delegation
- Slow decision-making
- Non-supportive spouse or family
- Unsustainable trend in negative cash flow
- Carrying people who aren't action-orientated
- 'Pimping the ride' – spending money on unnecessary items

Pathologies
- Cash flow unable to sustain company
- Loss of founder's commitment and interest

Action required
Companies in Infancy require a founder who can unite his or her people under a common cause and provide certainty in the face of overwhelming uncertainty and lack of clarity. The founder must be the repository for all fears; he or she must be strong, decisive and fair.

Infant companies need more of everything: sales, production, improvements, effort, focus … everyone in the company must be action-orientated and driven to produce results – there is no room to carry poor performers at this stage. The founder must lead by example and make strong decisions that move the company forward.

A founder must be careful not to give away too much equity just to get things going at this stage. You may live to regret this later on as you lose control and get stuck with people who aren't taking the company forward, so you end up carrying people who like riding the gravy train.

Infancy is not the time to create complicated financial models or sales forecasts, because things are changing so fast. These will waste your time – you will just be making things up, and in the process you could create a structure that might harm the business.

Moving on
- Company establishes products or services with key accounts
- Strong demand for products or services
- Consistent sales growth
- Healthy cash flow

Stage 3: Child
A Child organisation has a successful product or service, rapidly growing sales and a healthy cash flow. The company is growing fast and is thriving.

Like a child who has just learnt to walk, companies at this stage quickly get overconfident and start to believe that they are bullet proof. They think they can succeed at anything that comes their way.

The success of the Child is the initial realisation of the founder's dream. They start to think that if one dream can be achieved, then isn't anything possible? The founder is often 'chasing shiny pennies', pursuing any and all opportunities with a confidence and arrogance possessed only by those 'who cannot fail'.

Child companies are prone to rapid diversification and often end up spreading themselves too thin, because to them, more is always better. They don't focus enough on what matters and often end up losing money on their new ventures.

Companies at this stage have an insatiable appetite for growth and driving sales. The founder is single-minded in his or her approach, as this made him or her successful as an Infant, but in the Child phase it can make implementation of ideas difficult.

Management is often disorganised, as the founder hastily assigns work without adequate attention to what needs to be done. As a result, employees pursue uncertain assignments and, when they 'mess up', the founder takes this as evidence that if you need something done well, you need to do it yourself. This inability to effectively delegate will cause the founder to hold on too much, feeling trapped and becoming essential to every aspect of the business.

Accounting and metrics on the business are usually weak, and reporting is often so delayed that it is only of limited use to the company.

Employees are often frustrated due to high workloads and unclear responsibilities and goals. The infrastructure is often built as needed, rather than according to a longer-term plan, and can become unstable.

When things fall over for Child companies, as they invariably do, everyone places the blame with everyone else because of inadequate information and lack of authority, and the company can lose money quickly. The founder decides systems and policies are needed, so get their staff to make them, but the founder is often the first to violate them. The founder realises that centralised control doesn't provide the time needed to focus on the big picture, but decentralised leadership requires effective systems of control, which Child companies don't have. Founders yo-yo between handing work off to others, then taking it over again when it's not done to their liking. This frustrates both the founder and the employees.

Normal problems

- Sales-driven organisation
- Sales are viewed as more important than profits
- Reacting to opportunities rather than creating opportunities
- Unclear communication
- Everything is a priority
- Loose budgeting
- Ineffective management
- Reliance on the founder
- Confusion
- Frustrated employees
- Precarious infrastructure
- Crisis

Abnormal problems

- Blind arrogance of the founder
- Sustained lack of focus
- Consistent low quality
- Premature emphasis on profitability
- Total reliance on the founder
- No budgeting
- Leaders avoid managing in favour of doing
- Founder unwilling to hire people better than him or her
- No delegation and unwilling to delegate
- Key staff leave
- Collapsing infrastructure
- Major crisis

Pathologies

- Unable to develop the abilities needed to replace the founder
- Founder unwilling to delegate effectively
- Founder wants to stay involved in every decision

Action required

Flexibility is crucial for the success of the Child, and adding structure and control are crucial for the successful transition to Young Adult; this is a dynamic time for a company. To be successful, founders must change their attitude towards control, and this is often precipitated by a crisis caused by the company outgrowing its capabilities.

Another key part of the transition to Young Adult is for Child companies to focus on what's important and allocate resources appropriately.

Child companies require constant restructuring, and this is a lesson many entrepreneurs need to learn, because they created their success by breaking the rules and flipping the bird at structure. Founders must develop the skills, systems and trust to create a structure that supports decentralisation of control, and this starts with effective delegation. Delegation means moving tasks down the line to others, and when this is happening effectively, the much more challenging task of shifting some strategic decision-making away from the founder can begin. Make sure management is working effectively as a team.

Moving on
- Start delegating
- Commit to proper systems and controls, which is real decentralisation

Stage 4: Young Adult

Like a young adult person, a company in this phase comes into its own and must find a life apart from its founder (parents).

And, like a young adult person, the Young Adult years are a turbulent time for a company: sales fall short or production doesn't keep up with sales, new hires and old hands plot against each other, and quality might not be up to the customers' expectations. Morale can be volatile; some people love the changes, while others hate this time.

According to Dr Adizes, this is such a challenging transition for three reasons:

1. Decentralisation of authority.
2. Transition from entrepreneurial to professional leadership.
3. Evolution of company goals.

1. Decentralisation of authority: Moving from Child to Young Adult requires founders to relinquish their absolute power to professional management. This can be tough for founders who thrive on power and love being number one. Founders must learn to develop their people's abilities and decentralise control one step at a time. When they do this effectively, the professional manager will move into the space the founder creates. And it's important that, at the first sign of trouble, they don't leap in and take back control.

It's also crucial that the founder stays very involved in the company at this point and effectively delegates, not abdicates, to the new regime. The company still needs the founder, just in a different capacity.

2. Transition from entrepreneurial to professional leadership: Professional leadership is key to a successful transition, and there are a lot of challenges that go with this massive change in the company. The new leader must be given authority and not become a minion of the founder, or the new structure won't work. Their role is to make the company opportunity-driving rather than opportunity-driven, meaning they must put in place systems, processes, procedures, goals and compensation plans. They must do this carefully, as an over-emphasis on control can stagnate an entrepreneurial company that has thrived on high flexibility.

To make this phase a success, the founder must support and buy into the new initiatives, and he or she must also ensure that the new leader has parameters in which to operate so that the leader can make decisions and take actions that move the company in the right direction.

This is an emotional and challenging time for the founder and for the old-timers in the company, as well as the new professional leader, who has to implement a lot of change. This can also be an exhausting time for founders; what fuelled them in the early stages of the business – growth and sales – has been replaced by systems and de-centralisation of authority. A founder can feel a bit lost, but must stay focused on the ultimate goal of the company and not get bogged down.

3. Evolution of company goals: Young Adult companies need to change their goals from 'big is better' to 'better is better'. A focus on profitability is crucial to ensure that the company remains viable and sustainable over time.

This is not an easy evolution, and it involves an overhaul of the company structures, reporting and information, reward systems and resource allocation.

Normal problems
- Conflict and infighting
- Low morale
- Yo-yo delegation of authority
- Founder struggling to change leadership style
- Tired founder
- Upgrading of infrastructure
- Rising profits, flat sales
- Reduced importance placed on sales

Abnormal problems
- Permanent loss of trust
- Founder's refusal to change

- Exhausted founder
- Unchanging leadership and inability to decentralise
- Loss of critical staff
- Board's dismissal of founder
- Abdication of profit responsibility by the founder
- Excessive salaries to retain key staff
- Rising profits, falling sales
- Reduced investment in entrepreneurial development

Pathologies
- Inability to resolve conflict
- Founder gives up and disengages

Focusing internally all the energy that used to be directed externally to deal with the conflicts of the Young Adult phase can be a real drain on the company. If conflict isn't resolved it can result in a split, which leads to regression or stagnation.

A split where the founder fires the professional managers and regains control of the company will often cause a regression to the Child phase and the business will once again come to totally rely on the founder. This is a major step backwards.

In a split where the board fires the founder and the professional management takes over, the entrepreneurial spirit can be lost and the company can stagnate and not flourish. This is exactly what happened to Apple when Steve Jobs was fired.

When a founder gets so exhausted by the changing company, which doesn't feed their 'crack habit' of growth and sales, they can give up. This has the same effect as when the founder is fired by the board, but with the added complication of the team seeing someone they respected become someone they don't.

The best outcome is when the founder and the professional management resolve their differences and work together to grow the systems and structure and to maintain the entrepreneurial spirit.

Action required

To succeed as a Young Adult, companies need to introduce controls, strengthen infrastructure to create a scalable effective business, and do this in a way that enhances entrepreneurial spirit. Automation is a great way to accelerate growth, but be careful that automation is based on what is needed for the road ahead, not just on what is already happening.

Effective decentralisation of authority includes the entrepreneurial functions such as marketing, development, capitalisation and recruiting key staff; effectively, this is removing the over-dependency on the founder. The first step is to create a structure that is organised around these functions, not just around people.

The founder needs to learn to embrace delegation; this is key to avoid exhaustion. Think of it like an iPhone. You don't know how many apps it's running until you notice it's running out of battery really quickly, so you close some apps (that is, hand over some tasks) and recharge the battery. The phone gets back to normal speed and works well. Effective delegation results in the founder finding new energy and passion for his or her company, allowing him or her to contribute at an even higher level.

Getting clarity around the governance of the company and the roles, responsibilities and decision-making authority of the board and senior management is fundamental. The founder must then come to trust in the new system, and the employees must learn that they don't depend on the founder completely.

It is also important to clearly articulate the vision of the company, and get clear on the business it is in. The vision is no longer just held in the founder's head; everyone needs to understand it so everyone is pulling in the same direction.

Moving on
* Bring in a professional manager
* Invest time in the transition

As Dr Adizes says in *Managing Corporate Lifecycles*, 'Good management is not a marathon race. It is a relay race.' The professional management will move into the space vacated by the founder, so he or she can only be effective when the founder creates that space to hand over the baton.

Stage 5: Optimal
When a company has the infrastructure it needs to support current business and projected growth, and has institutionalised its entrepreneurial activities so it's no longer dependent on the founder to be successful, it enters the Optimal stage. A company is Optimal when it is operating at its best, and both growth and profitability are balanced, as are control and flexibility.

An Optimal company is guided by a vision that the team lives and breathes. Clear goals and priorities are set based on that vision, and the team is energised and excited about the future; staff love working at the company. Short-term gain is not favoured at the expense of a long-term relationship. Entrepreneurial functions have become institutionalised, and the organisation is a fertile breeding ground for controlled and profitable innovation, with structures and infrastructure working well. Clear governance allows employees to understand how decisions have been made. All opinions are respected, and there is healthy debate during decision-making. The company has consistent and market-beating growth in sales and profitability.

Normal problems
- Lack of management depth

Abnormal problems
- Lack of effective decentralisation
- Founder gets too comfortable
- Desire to stop innovating and maintain the status quo – lack of urgency
- Reliance on the past to guide the future
- Not getting out in front of customers

Pathologies
There are no normal problems in Optimal other than sometimes a lack of back-up for managers; any problem can lead to a decline. The first sign of decline is complacency and a lack of urgency.

Action required
Optimal is a state, not a destination, so the key is to maintain the balance between flexibility and control and to never get complacent. Management must keep up the entrepreneurial momentum by nurturing Infant, Child and Young Adult business units. The vitality of the organisation must be sustained or it will enter the Stable stage, which is the beginning of the decline.

Moving on
If enough energy and innovation isn't invested in the Optimal stage, a business enters gradual deterioration, and the stage it drops to

depends on the degree to which deterioration problems pervade the organisation.

Stage 6: Stable

The first sign of ageing is not seen in a company's financial statements, which can, in fact, look very healthy; it's seen in the attitudes and behaviours of the leaders. That's why Stable is at the top of the curve; it looks healthy, but it is not moving up any more. This is a very dangerous position to be in – according to McKinsey & Company, companies that grow at a rate slower than GDP are five times more likely to fail. Times are good, a sense of complacency creeps in and people lose the urgency and drive that got the company to Optimal. It's easy to get comfortable when you're driving a BMW and sitting in $2 000 chairs at mahogany desks!

While sales might be growing slowly, there is little or no growth of new product lines. The entrepreneurial parts of the business (marketing, sales and production) lose power to the corporate departments of finance, accounting, HR and legal, and the company becomes totally ruled by numbers and reports.

Saving yourself: If your business is Stable, then it's worth remembering that while you are patting yourself on the back, someone else is hungry and is working night and day to take your market share. Get your hunger back and recognise that this is the start of The Decline – which is not where you want to head if you want to be around in the future.

Stage 7: The Decline

Denial: A steady decline in flexibility becomes more obvious in Denial. While financial statements are strong, development is slowing and the company demonstrates little desire to conquer new markets or bring new products to market. People start to focus more on how something is done rather than the results it produces. In Denial the business is losing market share and, while individually people know this and it scares them, collectively they deny this reality and no one says anything about it.

To maintain their books, in Denial, businesses keep raising prices and cutting costs, but at some point this erodes all its hard-earned goodwill and the financial results start to look very unhealthy.

Saving yourself: Get honest and discuss the real problems. Denial is not a healthy state for a company to be in, but it doesn't have to be terminal. Reinvigorate the entrepreneurial spirit, invest in development, marketing and sales, and grow Infant, Child and Young Adult business units.

Blame: As the company slides into worse shape, the management team starts pointing fingers at each other and focusing on who caused the problems, not on what to do about them. The blame invariably falls on the entrepreneurial departments, and when the heads of these areas are fired, The Decline speeds up.

Saving yourself: Step up, take accountability, figure out the problem and solve it. In Blame, you must invest in the entrepreneurial departments.

Fiction: The company gets a breath of life when an external force, usually in the form of government, wants to keep it alive. For most companies there is no external force to keep them alive, so they skip this step and go straight to Death. Fiction runs on systems for the sake of systems and there is no pressure to perform. Because the company relies on political handouts, it can die as soon as the handouts stop.

Saving yourself: This is a really tenuous position to be in and requires massive change to save the company. It will take a very strong leader who is totally committed to a complete reorganisation and reinvigoration of the company.

Death: When the money runs out and the handouts stop, the company dies. At this stage, the best you can do is try to sell the assets before the liquidators take over.

SUMMARY

If you are reading this book, it is highly likely your company is on the upward side of the slope.

Maybe you're Flirting with a cool idea and you're looking to make it a reality.

You might be looking to grow your Infant's consistent sales and increase demand for your product or service.

You might have a thriving Child and you've identified the need for systems and to start delegating some of your workload.

You might have an unruly Young Adult and you've established that you'll only reach the next level with professional management.

You might have an Optimal business and you've realised that you need to keep investing energy into your company to make it even better.

Or you might be at the top of the curve, and your company is in a Stable state. While times are good, there's a niggle telling you that danger is on the horizon. This is a perfect time to get excited about your company again and to invest the same energy into it that got it to where it is.

Or, alternatively, you've identified that you're on the downward side of the curve. Now is the perfect time to step up and be accountable, to identify the problem, to create solutions, and to implement those solutions and make your company great again.

Remember, what got you to where you are now isn't going to get you to where you want to go – you're going to have to do things differently. With an understanding of the life cycle of a business, you are now much better positioned to know exactly what it is you might need to do differently. So I encourage you to lean into the change and take your business to the next step – don't stay where you are and stagnate.

In business, as in life, you're either growing or you're dying – there is no in between. So make sure that you commit to growth, to constant and never-ending improvement, to accountability and leaning into the challenge, and to creating a great business.

When you do this, there is nothing that can stop you.

THE 12 ROUNDS OF
THE UNFAIR FIGHT

Like a boxing match, this book also consists of 12 rounds.

Because being in business can be a bit like being in the ring with Mike Tyson, the path to creating success is also similar to a boxing match. By now you've identified where your business and industry are in their life cyles, so now is the time to learn and apply the Unfair Fight.

I've divided this into three parts because, in business, like in a fight, there is the set-up where you prepare and ready yourself to do battle; there is the actual fight, where you roll up your sleeves and get into your work, literally fighting for your life; and there is the opportunity to go for the knockout, the killer blow that no one can defend themselves against.

Get these three parts right and you will have created an incredibly successful, and profitable, business.

PART 1: THE SET-UP

First, there's the set-up. The fight starts with you. If you're not in a powerful state, then the fight's over before it's begun. The first four rounds are your training, what you need to do to be the strongest when you get into the ring.

Round 1 – Decide

Round 2 – Love

Round 3 – Mind Bullets

Round 4 – Leadership

PART 2: THE FIGHT

Once you are the best you can be, it's time to step into the ring and get into the guts of the fight. Here, you have to do the right things at the right times, knowing what combination to throw, when to attack and when to defend. How to do this is covered in the next six rounds.

Round 5 – Differentiation

Round 6 – Results Marketing

Round 7 – New Sales

Round 8 – Culture and Team

Round 9 – Planning for Results

Round 10 – Execution

PART 3: THE KNOCKOUT

And, finally, you are the best that you can be; you can do the work, but to win gloriously, you have to deliver the knockout punch. While you might be surprised by what this book reveals as the knockout blow, it will become your secret weapon in creating incredible business success.

Round 11 – Stacking Your Corner

Round 12 – The Power of Questions

When you put it all together by being the best you can be, then doing the right things at the right times, then delivering the knockout blow, you will create a business that doesn't just survive, but thrives.

Let's start this journey together, now.

PART 1

The Set-up

The most important part of any fight is *you*: how you show up, how you engage and the habits that you adopt.

Business success is no different. If you just focus on the techniques – what you have to do – you will miss the single most important factor that determines your success or failure: you.

The first four rounds are dedicated to the most important and most powerful ways that you can create the best you.

The biggest chokehold on any business is the psychology of the owner. Many books make the process of creating a success psychology complicated, but it doesn't have to be. Just follow the action steps in the next four chapters and watch the massive impact it has on your life, and your business.

Remove the limits that your psychology has been placing on your business, step up as the leader your business is calling for, and anything's possible.

Please don't rush through Part 1 because you are so keen to get into the 'how to'. Start at the beginning, because what you'll learn here is the ultimate difference between success and failure.

ROUND 1

Decide

The Latin root of the word 'decide' means 'to cut off'. To make a real decision is to cut off all other possibilities.

When you decide that success is yours, it is.

Round 1 of the Unfair Fight is about you making a decision. It is also about you recognising the three decisions that are shaping your life and your business, and how you can direct those decisions to create the destiny and business of your choice. This is the shortest chapter *and it is also the most important*. If this chapter is all you take from this book, then you are already at a massive advantage.

The quality of your life is a direct reflection of the quality of your decisions.

THE POWER OF A SINGLE DECISION …

At its height in 1519, the Aztec Empire covered some 20 000 square kilometres in central and southern Mexico and ruled between five and six million people. That year, the Spanish conquistador Hernán Cortés arrived with the aim of overthrowing this vast empire. He brought with him just 500 soldiers and 13 horses. Not exactly a large army, or at least not one likely to be feared by what was then the western hemisphere's most powerful nation.

They were massively outnumbered and the men were terrified, and Cortés knew he had to take definitive action. So when he and his army landed on the shore, he told his men: 'Burn the boats.'

Cortés said that by burning the boats they would conquer the Aztec army and gain their fortune. Cortés wanted his men to understand fully that their only option was to win or die – there would be no retreat, no in between, no back-up plan.

Their only option was to take the Aztecs' boats home.

Too often, we give ourselves a back-up plan, an 'out'. We want to make sure that we have something to fall back on if things go wrong. But the problem is that by giving yourself a back-up plan, that actually *becomes* the plan.

When faced with a risk, you must eliminate any obstacles that might hold you back from giving your full effort. If you know that you have an escape plan, are you really going to shoot for success with as much effort as if this was your last and only hope?

If your life literally depended on it, how much effort would you put in?

Have you ever had those conversations in your head? 'If this doesn't work, I can always get my old job back.' 'If I don't like university, I can always go home to Mom and Dad.' 'If this marriage doesn't work, I can always get a divorce.'

This attitude almost always leads to failure. It holds no power.

The fighter who, in Round 1, is considering what they'll say to their friends and family when they lose is unlikely ever to make it to Round 2. Muhammad Ali did not say, 'Float like a butterfly, sting like a bee … if I lose I'll go home and watch *The Simpsons*.'

Having a great fight starts with you being an effective fighter – it starts with you.

But back to the Aztecs. The message Cortés sent was not just intended for his army. After word spread of his definitive actions on the beach, the Aztecs knew that the Spanish were literally fighting for their lives. The Aztecs understood that they would be unable to force the Spanish to retreat because there was nowhere for the invaders to go. On the other hand, with an entire empire behind them, the Aztec forces would always be aware of their own option to retreat. In the face of the Spanish commitment to total victory, the Aztecs would themselves be more inclined to retreat and less inclined to fight hard to hold ground.

Cortés's men were totally focused and motivated. They didn't just *want* to win, they *needed* to win in order to survive.

By 1521, just two years later, Cortés and his small army had conquered the Aztecs.

So the question for you is this:

Do I choose success?

Are you prepared to 'burn your boats' and give your business your total dedication and focus? Are you prepared to do whatever it takes to succeed? Are you ready to decide that success, not failure, is your destiny?

Are you prepared to read this book and apply what you learn? Relentlessly?

Please don't just read this chapter, say 'Yes', and move on. Take the time to consider these questions and your answers. Because a 'Yes' that hasn't been thought through is not a decision at all. Success means a commitment from your entire being.

That being said, making this decision doesn't have to take long. If you can truthfully answer 'Yes', then you are already one of the minority of people who *do*, versus the majority who just *talk* about it.

BURNING YOUR BOATS

When Cortés instructed his men to burn their boats, he knew that in order to defeat a much larger army, he needed superior leverage; he needed to be able to do more with less. Similarly, you can create the leverage you need to be successful.

Get clear about what success means for you. Be very careful here that you are honest about what success looks like ideally, not what it looks like safely. What would success look like if you knew you couldn't fail?

Determine and record 'why' success is a must for you. What will it mean for you and your family when you achieve it? What would it cost you not to achieve it? By being brutally honest in both these areas, you will create a pull towards your goal and a drive away from what you don't want.

1. Make the decision to choose success.
2. Increase leverage by sharing your commitment with someone whose opinion you value and who will hold you accountable – today.
3. Remind yourself of your decision daily and take action towards your desired outcome.

For more on decision-making, access the Decision Worksheet by registering at www.samhazledine.com.

That's it. While this first step might seem insignificant, it is the most important, and critical in setting you up for the Unfair Fight. Choosing success allows you to draw from the depths of your true power and access all the resources available to you when retreat is not an option.

You'll create success like your life depends on it.

Because it does.

You'll move from wanting success to needing it, and that's exactly where you need to be.

As I've said, when I started MedRecruit I had no business experience. I was also entering a market dominated by a company with a monopoly. I realised that I would need to turn up with everything I had, that I could leave nothing in the tank.

I realised that to create success, I had to *decide* to create success and to commit to it with everything I had.

I got very clear on what sort of business I wanted to create: an internationally successful company that would transform the status quo of its industry and provide doctors with the lifestyles they wanted in medicine, and hospitals with the certainty they needed in their staffing.

I realised that I had to remove all my 'outs'. I couldn't go into this with a back-up plan. For me, the success of MedRecruit was all or nothing, and I was either going to create a massively successful business or I was going to die trying.

That total commitment, that total dedication to developing my vision and removing any form of a back-up plan meant that, when times were tough, I had no option but to persist and think creatively to find a way through. It meant that I worked as hard as I needed to, and more, to evolve my company into an internationally recognised brand with a massive positive impact on the medical recruitment industry.

I didn't just want success, I needed it. My future depended on it. So does yours.

THREE DECISIONS THAT SHAPE YOUR LIFE

Once you have decided that success is your destiny, that it's a need not just a want, you have to understand the three decisions that are constantly shaping your life and your future, in both your personal life and your business. When you are unaware of these decisions, you are 'at effect' in your life; when you become aware of and direct them, you are 'at cause'.

Anthony Robbins, the well-known life coach and motivational speaker, initially taught me about the power of decisions, and this idea has shaped my entire life and business, and continues to shape it daily. *A decision is a cause set in motion.*

1. What do I decide to focus on?

Where you put your intention, your focus, is what will be real for you. By deciding what to focus on, you are deciding where you are going to direct your energy, and hence you are deciding what direction you want to go in.

Are you focusing on the past, the present or the future? Are you focusing on yourself or on others? Are you focusing on the opportunities or the limitations? Are you focusing on the resources you don't have available to you or on your resourcefulness and everything that *is* available to you? There are patterns of focus and you need to become aware of yours, because as soon as you are aware, you will know whether your focus is serving you well or whether it needs to be redirected.

2. What meaning do I decide to give to this?

You have the power to decide what meaning you will give to any situation. Emotion comes from the meaning you give to any one thing or any experience, and emotion is the fuel of life. The events of our life are not what are important; what is important is the meaning we attach to those events. *Meaning is a choice.*

Meaning is not thrust upon you; it's a decision you make.

Two people can experience the same event and choose to focus on different things, therefore choosing to give the event different meanings. Two business owners could trade themselves into insolvency, and one could decide that that means he isn't cut out for business, while the other could decide that she is learning lessons that are invaluable towards becoming a titan of business.

Are you going to give the events of your life empowering meanings or disempowering meanings? Does something mean the end or the beginning? Is the situation here to punish you or to serve you? Do you see it as a blockage or a test?

3. What action do I decide to take?

Deciding what you focus on and what that means to you shapes the emotions you feel and therefore the decisions you make and the actions you take.

In the previous example of the two insolvent business owners, the one who decided insolvency meant he wasn't cut out for business might give up; the one who decided that the lessons learnt were invaluable might decide to do whatever it takes, to learn whatever she needs to learn, to work harder than she has ever worked before and to trade out of insolvency and to create a great company.

That's what I did in the early days, when I traded my company MedRecruit into insolvency and then out. Some of the most powerful lessons in *Winning the Unfair Fight* come directly from having my back to the wall and giving myself no choice but to think creatively and come up with resourceful ways to do more with less.

What you focus on and the meaning you give it is only important to the extent of its impact on the actions you take.

In every moment of your life, in every moment of your business, you are deciding what to focus on, what that means and what you are going to do.

SIX COMMITMENTS TO CREATE YOUR DESTINY

The outcome of a decision is a commitment. The difference between people who fail to get the results they desire in life and business and those who get what they want is the difference between being interested and being committed.

People who are interested in success, in achieving what they want, will achieve it if it's convenient, and it usually isn't, so they don't.

On the other hand, people who are committed will do what they need to do to achieve what's important to them. Full stop.

Someone who's interested in getting fit will wake up, see that it is raining and go back to bed. Someone who's committed will wake up, see that it is raining and put on a raincoat.

To master the Unfair Fight, you will need to make these six commitments. The Unfair Fight will be of some use if you are interested in business success, and it will be invaluable if you are committed.

1. I am committed to action

Knowledge isn't power; *knowledge with action* is power. Successful people are committed not only to learning, but to implementing and taking massive action.

Every time you learn something valuable in this book, take action. Don't worry about getting it perfect, but do worry about getting it done.

> 'The man who is waiting for something
> to turn up might start on his shirtsleeves.'
> — GARTH HENRICHS

2. I am committed to speed

Successful entrepreneurs and business owners take action fast. They don't see failure as the end; rather, they see it as a necessary part of learning and success.

The world, and business, is moving quickly and one of the biggest reasons businesses fail is because the owner is too slow.

Speed plus the right strategy equals success. This book will give you the strategies to take effective action quickly.

3. I am committed to doing whatever it takes

'If at first you don't succeed, try, try and try again.' If a child is learning to walk, how many times do you make sure they try until they succeed?

As many times as it takes.

Children try as often as they need to until they learn to walk, to ride a bike, to swim … and so on. Adults encourage their kids to never give up, so why don't more adults apply that approach to their own lives?

You never give up on them, so why would you give up on yourself?

Taking action alone isn't enough. You must make the commitment to yourself that you will persist and do whatever it takes, without harming others, to achieve your ultimate outcome, to become successful. Getting results is your focus, not the process. Be committed to your outcome and remain flexible in your approach, because achieving success is a dynamic process.

The secret of achieving success in anything is to get up more times than you fall over. If you fail 1 000 times, then to be successful you just need to try 1 001 times. It's not complicated.

People who achieve success are people who practise; they know they won't be the best when they start out, so they commit to practising until they become brilliant. Aim to get to 'unconscious competence', where you are so good at the important areas in your life that you don't even have to think about them. Commit to this, and you will be unstoppable.

4. I am committed to taking total responsibility for my results

There is only one person you ultimately have control over: yourself. Successful people adopt the belief that the conditions of their lives are their responsibility.

Put another way, successful people take charge of their lives.

It is incredibly powerful to take ownership of your life and your business, and to stop making excuses and giving others the power.

It's time for you to step up and own the conditions of your life. Now.

5. I am committed to stretching

Your ultimate destiny lies just outside the limits of your comfort zone. To achieve your potential, to create the life of your dreams, to create the business you always dreamt of, you must commit to continuing to stretch yourself.

Lean into the discomfort.

As you learn new things that will benefit you, lean into them. Don't be afraid if you don't get it right the first time.

Muscles grow when they are stretched to their limits and break, then they rebuild themselves even stronger. It is important that you do the same in your life.

6. I am committed to acting with personal integrity

Integrity means being true to your values and ensuring that what is on the outside is the same as what is on the inside.

Get clear about your beliefs and values, and see that they are in alignment with what you want to achieve.

If you value creating a global business that impacts the lives of millions, and you also value sleeping until midday and then watching TV all afternoon, then you might have a problem.

Review your values and make sure that they are helping you achieve your target.

Access the Commitments Worksheet at www.samhazledine.com to increase the leverage you have on yourself to make these commitments.

CHOOSE WISELY

Decisions shape your life and, ultimately, your destiny, every moment of every day. Be aware of the decisions you are making and ensure that these decisions take you in the direction you want to go in.

Decide to be successful, and you will be.

*Decide where to focus, and make sure this
moves you in the direction you want.*

*Decide what meaning you will attach to the events in your life,
and make that meaning powerful.*

*Decide what you are going to do to move towards your ultimate
destiny, and make the commitments you need in order to achieve it.*

Essentially, your motto must be:

*If I want to create an exceptional business, then I
must be committed to creating an exceptional business.*

In my experience, the majority of people are not consciously making these four decisions or the necessary commitments. By consciously making these decisions, you are tapping into the power of being 'at cause' in your life.

Armed with these four decisions, you will give yourself an unassailable advantage.

That's the Unfair Fight.

ROUND 2

Love

When I ask most business owners, or aspiring business owners, why they want to be in business, there are a range of answers. Most are along the lines of: 'I don't want to work for someone else and I want to create a great lifestyle for myself.'

Most of these people are destined to be knocked out in an early round, or at best create a very mediocre business that is much harder than just working for someone else.

These people are in business for the money and the lifestyle that it will provide. While you want to keep money in your head, you don't want money in your heart. Ironically, if money is in your heart as your primary driver, you are most likely destined to struggle financially, while if it's in your head, you are more likely to be financially successful.

> *'Choose a job you love, and you will*
> *never have to work a day in your life.'*
> — CONFUCIUS

This trips up a lot of business owners. Is it tripping you up now?

If you are getting in the ring, it's important you want to *be* in the ring, that *you love being in the ring.*

> *'A rooster crows only when it sees the light. Put him in the dark and he'll never crow. I have seen the light and I'm crowing.'*
> — MUHAMMAD ALI

There's absolutely nothing wrong with wanting autonomy and financial freedom and all that that gives you. *I* certainly do. But those can't be your only reasons for being in business – they have little power, because nobody cares what you want.

It might seem strange that the second most important round of the Unfair Fight is *Love*, but the reality is that without love, you are likely to fail, as do most people.

The physical expression of love is passion, and passion is fundamental to business success, because business can be so hard. In business you have to perform over a sustained period of time – there is no 'overnight success'. One truth I've learnt is that it takes a long time to become an overnight success.

Successful people love their business on a number of levels, and this attitude is critical to persevering with the challenges that are a daily part of being in business. The business owners who don't love it will quit. Who could put up with so much hard work and constant worry over such a long period of time if you didn't love it? You can't. It's just not possible for sane people – unless they're in love.

I liken this passion to having a child: who would put up with the sleepless nights, the constant attention, the worry, if they didn't love that little rascal more than life itself?

You can love the business, the product or service, and the people. Preferably you love all three, starting with the people.

SWITCHING FROM LOVING THE PRODUCT TO LOVING THE PEOPLE

'You will get all you want in life if you help
enough other people get what they want.'

— ZIG ZIGLAR

Who are the people involved in your business? There are two key groups of people in any business: your staff and your customers.

As a business owner, it's certainly preferable to have a better product or provide a better service than anyone else. And it's essential to keep in mind whom you're doing that for. If it's primarily to provide you with the things you want, then you're in trouble. It's your customers who put food on your table and it's your staff who make it happen.

The market doesn't exist to provide for you; you exist to provide for the market.

Let me ask you a question: Who do you think is the most important person or group of people in your business?

Some people will say themselves, many will say the customer, and a few will say their staff.

I believe the best answer is your staff, followed by your customers, followed by you.

'But the customer is always right,' I hear you saying. That's one of the stupidest sayings in business, one that causes business owners to chase their tails and pander to the needs of a few 'squeaky wheels' rather than focusing on the people who make the biggest difference. Of course the customer is important, of course they must be listened to, and of course you need to do what you can to provide them with a great product or service.

But always right? No way.

No one is *always* right, and that includes your customers.

Loving your staff

For every staff member there are hundreds, potentially thousands, of customers. When you look at it that way, it makes sense that your employees are by far the most important people in your business. Round 8 deals directly with people and culture, and how to make sure your employees feel the love. It also tells you how to create a culture that the competition can't improve on (see pages 214–216).

But for now, start by remembering that your employees have a choice and, at the moment, they are choosing to work for you. Be incredibly grateful that these wonderful and talented people give the majority of their waking hours to work towards your vision for your company.

I think that's pretty cool, and it's an incredible privilege to be an employer.

When you keep that in mind, it's not hard to love your staff. They are awesome. When you remember this, you will focus not just on what they can do for you, but what you can do for them, how you can help them to get more of what they want in life.

When your employees are more fulfilled in their work and they are also achieving what's important to them in life, they will be loyal to you and will demand more of themselves than you could ever demand of them.

So don't keep your love to yourself. Make sure that they know you appreciate them. One of the most powerful things I've learnt is to appreciate my employees. It's not just about what they've achieved for your business, it's about genuinely appreciating them for who they are.

One of the other things that I've found that really serves my employees and lets them know that I care about them is to help them achieve what's important in their lives. I run personal development sessions every month to help them to grow, and we run a yearly Goal Achievement Programme to help them both personally and professionally. I get unbelievable feedback from my team about these sessions, and I get a real thrill seeing the great things they go on to accomplish.

When you go into battle, as you do every day in business, you need people on your side who know they are appreciated, because then they will be loyal and will do whatever it takes for your business.

Loving your customers

All businesses have to provide a product or a service, but you aren't providing this just because you want to. You're providing it to make a difference in the lives of the people who buy it – your customers. Remember, the market doesn't exist to provide for you, you exist to provide for the market.

Loving your customers means that you focus on the benefits that your product provides, not on its features. You focus on the difference your product can make in the lives of the people who use it. You focus on creating a business-model advantage from their perspective, not yours.

Remember that everything you want in life is available if you give enough other people what they want. So love those people you are serving, focus on their needs and wants, then focus on exceeding those needs and wants. When you do that, you will have an unfair advantage over your competition, who are focusing on their product.

By delivering on their needs consistently, you will create loyal customers. Customers who know they are loved and whose needs are consistently exceeded are loyal.

Here are some great inexpensive ways to show your customers that you love them:
- Write them a personal card.
- Call them and say, 'Thank you, I appreciate you.'
- Learn and remember the little things: their birthdays, their kids' names, their hobbies, etcetera.

You don't need to be perfect at this, but do start. Call a customer today and say, 'I appreciate you,' and see what happens.

Loving your business

Your business is like having a child – it needs constant love, attention and nourishment from you.

Personally I love business, and I love *my* business. I thrill at the challenges it presents me. I relish overcoming those challenges. And I love the results the business creates for my employees, my customers, and for my family and me.

I think it's hard to be successful in business unless you love your business. If you don't, then you'll continually shift your attention to the things you do love, and your business will falter. It's just human nature to gravitate towards the things we love.

I encourage you to find what it is that you love about business in general, and what you love about your business in particular. Remind yourself of those things when the times are tough because, as I said before, passion is the physical expression of love and you must be passionate to get yourself, your staff and your business through the inevitable challenges of being in business.

A VISION THAT INSPIRES

People want to be inspired, and most people look to leaders to get inspiration. A great way to inspire people is to give them a vision to believe in and to work towards. A vision will focus your team on heading in the right direction.

A vision gives your staff something to base their daily activities around and to guide them in the creation of strategies and tactics.

For a vision to inspire, it needs to be about passion and it needs to be about the people.

Most business owners fail to have a clearly defined vision, and if there's no love for what they do, then there's no vision.

Of those who do have a vision, the majority will focus it on 'what' their business does. For MedRecruit, the 'what' might look like this: 'To provide the best-matched placements of doctors in hospitals.'

Hey, it's what we do. But putting it this way sounds about as inspiring as the thought of drinking a cold fish milkshake.

So take it a step further and have a vision about 'how' your business will achieve its results.

The MedRecruit example might be: 'To provide a service that makes it easy for doctors to find jobs that meet their career, lifestyle and financial goals.'

That sounds much better, but it's still a fish milkshake, this time with a dash of vodka to make it more palatable.

The best visions, the ones that really have the power to move people, are about 'why' the business exists. Your business's 'why' is its reason for existing – it's why your business continues to have a heartbeat.

For MedRecruit, our vision is: 'Enrich Lives'.

It's that simple. That's 'why' we exist. It's why we've always existed. And it's why we are successful.

We enrich the lives of our employees; they grow personally and professionally by being part of the company, and we reward them well.

We enrich the lives of our doctors; they are happy in their work, with what they are earning and with their lifestyle. They are making their careers work for them, rather than just slogging away in the system.

We enrich the lives of the hospital recruitment staff; we make their lives easier by giving them the doctors they need when they need them, and we always aim to brighten their day in what can be a very challenging job.

And we ultimately enrich the lives of the patients who are treated by our doctors. Happy doctors are less stressed, and less-stressed doctors make fewer mistakes, and fewer mistakes lead to better patient outcomes.

As you can see, our vision isn't complicated. It's not a three-page manifesto that no one understands. It's simply 'why' we are in business. When you reflect on the essence of what you do, it becomes obvious. It's easy for anyone to understand, and everyone in your organisation will know why you do what you do. The purpose of a vision is to focus your team in the right direction every day.

Exercise

1. Map out your business:
   a. 'What' you produce.
   b. 'How' you produce it.
   c. 'Why' you produce it.
2. Create a simple vision based on 'why' your business exists.
3. Share it with your team and make it part of the everyday conversation.

Access the Vision Worksheet by registering at
www.samhazledine.com.

A MISSION THAT MOVES

What business are you *really* in?

This is one of the most powerful questions you can ask about your business.

Most people think that the answer to this question is the industry they are in: recruitment, professional services, hospitality, tourism, widgets, etcetera.

But the industry isn't what business you are in.

Customers buy on emotion and justify with logic. So you need to figure out the primary emotion the majority of your customers get from buying your product or using your service. When you figure out this emotion, you can tailor your entire business towards it – then you really are using the Unfair Fight, because your customers will come back again and again. You've given them what they really want, and your competition will have no idea what's hit them.

I love personal development. I love learning new things and I love pushing myself and getting outside of my comfort zone.

But just because I love it doesn't mean it's for everyone.

A massive mistake I made was confusing what I wanted with what my customers wanted. It's a common mistake. My business and our brand became all about growth: it was loud, it was out there – and it was missing the mark in a big way. After wondering what wasn't working, we did something quite mind-boggling; we actually talked to our doctors and found that the reason they loved our service had nothing to do with what *I* loved. They loved dealing with us because they saw us as the best chance of getting the work they wanted, and they loved the high-quality personal service that they knew they would get every time.

Essentially, they were coming to us for the certainty of getting the work they wanted.

When we realised that the emotion our business primarily needed to provide was 'certainty', it dramatically changed how we operated and how we positioned the company. And the company grew rapidly.

Exercise

1. Talk to your customers and ask them why they use your product or service. Keep asking 'why' until you get to the *emotional reason* they choose you.
2. Look at all the answers you have and determine the underlying theme.

3. Determine what emotion that theme represents – *that's* the business you're in.
4. Review your entire business, including marketing, sales and service, and determine how you can provide that core emotion at every point where you have contact with customers.

When you give people what they really want, the emotion they are truly seeking, they will come back again and again because it's addictive.

SUMMARY

When you love your staff, your customers, your product or service, and your business, you will have incredible passion not just for what you do or how you do it, but also for why you really are in business. This will not only inspire your staff and your customers, but it will also inspire you, and give you the determination and energy to get through the tough times that are inevitable in any business.

You will tap into a power that very few business owners ever do and, by doing that, you will have the fuel necessary for the Unfair Fight. Almost certainly your competition won't be doing this because, in my experience, the majority of businesses don't have a vision or are too focused on the 'what' or 'how' of their business and miss the point of 'why' they exist.

The simple formula for business success is to figure out 'why' you exist and the emotion that your customers are craving from you. Then develop your business with that emotion in mind and give it to your customers.

It's that simple.

ROUND 3

Mind Bullets

As I shared at the start of the book, in 2002 I sustained a life-threatening head injury that was a direct result of my own reckless behaviour. I was in a coma for a couple of days and the doctors didn't expect me to make a full recovery; they thought I wouldn't regain full brain function. Their prognosis was that I would be unlikely to return to medical school, and I would never ski again.

After that terrible prognosis, I realised that I needed to raise my standards in life. I had to raise the bar just to get back to normal, and the lessons I learnt doing that taught me that I could raise the bar and keep raising it. I was forced to grow.

I believe that the purpose of setting goals is not just to achieve those goals; it is to become the person you need to be to achieve those goals. To become the person you need to be, you first have to develop a powerful psychology, a way to direct your mind, with sniper-like accuracy, at excellence in your life. I call this strategy 'mind bullets'. When you effectively think like this, then no matter what happens in life, you can find a way to succeed.

Remember, business success happens at the intersection of mindset and action.

When you want to change your life it's rarely a question of your capability; it's almost always a question of your motivation — how much you really want it.

And when your motivation is high, it then becomes a question of your effectiveness.

So the question for you is: Who do you need to become to achieve the success you want and deserve in business, and in life?

And how badly do you want it?

Almost everyone gets this wrong because they spend too much time focusing on 'What do I need to do?', so they miss the 'Who do I need to be?' It's like planning a journey by only focusing on the map and neglecting the fact that you need a car to drive there.

The Unfair Fight is about becoming the person you need to be and developing your psychological 'mind bullets', so failure is not an option.

Knowing who you need to be is truly powerful.

Becoming that person is not as complicated as many of the self-help books make it out to be. Don't buy into the common thinking that this process needs to be difficult. If you master some core strategies, you will be at a massive advantage.

You will then move well beyond competing with the big corporates, because no one in those companies will care as much as you do; no one will turn up with the same intensity as you. Turn up to their knife fight with the mental equivalent of an AK-47.

You will be living the Unfair Fight.

> *'You only live once, but if you do it right, once is enough.'*
> — MAE WEST

HOW THE BRAIN WORKS

It's important to understand the basics of how your mind and brain work to be able to use them to their full potential. If you were a race-car driver, you'd want to at least have a general understanding of the mechanics of a car before you raced it, wouldn't you?

I trained as a doctor, and while I've read countless confusing books about how the brain works, it's actually quite simple. I'll reveal exactly what you need to know, without the complicated mumbo-jumbo.

Put simply, we have a conscious mind and a subconscious mind. The subconscious mind is estimated to be over 30 000 times more powerful than our conscious mind, so while you might think you are consciously calling the shots, think again; there's a much more powerful force at work.

The subconscious mind cannot make choices or value judgements; it merely obeys your dominant thoughts. This is why you invariably get what you focus on; by focusing on something, you are telling your subconscious to 'pay attention, this is important to me'.

In addition, the mind has been shown to emit energy. In a talk I heard by Jack Canfield, author of *Chicken Soup for the Soul*, he shared an experiment conducted by NASA, where astronauts in space looked at different shapes, and then people meditating on the ground in America would say what shape they were looking at. They got it right much more than was statistically possible by chance. The astronauts' minds sent information in the form of energy across space. Just think about that power.

Every thought you have is sending out a message: it's paving the road ahead of you, it's telling people what to think and how to interact when they meet you, it's shaping your future.

Claire and I went to Paris on our honeymoon. Before we left on our trip, some people told us Parisians were unfriendly and unpleasant to foreigners who didn't speak good French. We didn't believe this and went there expecting to meet wonderful people who lived in a wonderful city, and that's exactly what happened. Parisians were gracious and friendly and we had a great time communicating in our very limited French; in fact, our terrible French led to a lot of fun and laughter with our new Parisian friends – there's only so many times you can order baguettes and ask directions to the library! Our positive thoughts paved the way for us, just as the thoughts of people who thought Parisians were unfriendly paved the way for them.

Albert Einstein stated that the most important decision that any person makes is whether he or she lives in a friendly or hostile universe – it's your choice.

Having this attitude is great, because it allows you to harness an incredibly powerful resource. But it can also bite you if you aren't in control of your focus. For example, if you are worrying about money and getting rid of your debt, then your subconscious just hears 'debt' and 'money worries'. It doesn't hear the 'I don't want' part, because it just focuses on the topic of the thought, not whether you like it or not. So, while you don't want the debt and you are worried about money, you have inadvertently set the sights of your subconscious on the debt and money worries, and it pulls you in that direction. I call this negative goal-setting, and it is killing the dreams of so many people.

On the other hand, if you have a lot of debt right now and not a lot of money, but you decide to focus on what you are going to create and the abundance that will bring to your life, rather than the debt, then you set the sights of your incredibly powerful subconscious on what you want – abundance. It becomes an ally to move you in that direction. I call this positive goal-setting, and this allows people to achieve the exceptional.

You need to become vigilant about your thoughts, knowing those thoughts are sending out energy and paving the way for you, and you also need to be vigilant about the information you are absorbing. Both are shaping your life as surely as a sculptor shapes a formless piece of marble into a beautiful statue, or a demolition man reduces an old piece of furniture to splinters. Your mind is capable of taking you to the absolute pinnacle, and it can also put you in the gutter.

Think of your mind like an iceberg, with the conscious mind being the small part above the water, and the subconscious as the majority below the water. It doesn't matter how much the bit above the water 'wants' to move north, if the current is flowing south, that's the direction it's going. The key to moving in the direction you want is to set your sights on north, and then turn the current to north too.

This is exactly what this chapter will reveal – how to turn the current to go in the direction you want it to go. It's actually not that hard, but it is incredibly powerful.

Then you'll have a resource 30 000 times stronger than your competition. That'll help, don't you think?

FLIPPING THE MODEL OF ACHIEVEMENT

When it comes to achieving outcomes, most people approach this in completely the wrong way. They start with 'What do I have to do?', get totally lost in their to-do lists and end up mistaking activity for achievement. Then they end up spinning their wheels and not making the progress they want, which leads to worry and negative goal-setting.

To be effective, you need to start with clarity by answering the question: 'What do I really want?' Your answer will focus you in the direction you want to go.

To engage your full emotional resources, you need to not just focus on what you want, but also 'why' the outcome is important to you. With a strong enough 'why', the 'how' will always reveal itself.

You then have to believe that you *can* make it happen and that you *will* make it happen; belief is critical.

Then you need to activate yourself, which means getting yourself up to full power, mobilising all your resources.

THE MODEL OF ACHIEVEMENT

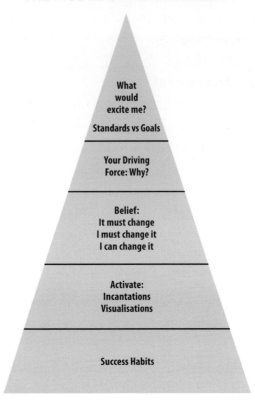

After you have completed these steps, then, and only then, do you work out what you need to do.

By beginning with the end in mind, you set yourself up for success.

1. CLARITY ON OUTCOMES

Getting clear about what you want is the first step to developing a powerful psychology and harnessing the power of your subconscious mind.

But all outcomes are not created equal.

It takes no more time to think big than it does to think small, so allow yourself to think as big as you want, but don't think *bigger* than you want, because you don't have to.

Three levels of outcomes

There are three levels of outcomes. They are created by answering three very different questions:

1. What can I achieve safely?

In my experience, this is the level at which most people live. The answer to this question creates outcomes that have very little power to move you, and certainly don't cause you to create excellence or great success in your life. These are all about playing safe. Usually you are quite ambivalent about these outcomes, so even though they are not a stretch, you still fail to achieve them.

2. What would I like to achieve?

This pushes you a little further and begins to take you outside your comfort zone. The big problem here is that as you start to move outside your comfort zone, you also start to move away from the people close to you. And because these outcomes aren't really exciting, and therefore lack real power, the pull from your peers is usually stronger than the pull from the outcome, and you end up back where you were.

3. What would excite me?

This is where things get interesting. This is where you dare to dream. This is where you create outcomes that truly move you to the depths of your being, that have the power to draw from everything you have. These outcomes are much stronger than the pull from your peers and they harness the power of your subconscious. They turn the tide in your favour, and they move you forward.

You get to choose which level of outcome you will achieve in your life, and therefore how much power it will have. This is a massive advantage, because the big corporates you are competing against almost always set their outcomes based on what they can achieve safely, with a small budget for what they would like to achieve. They almost never set their outcomes based on what would excite them; it's not safe enough.

This is where you can easily outgun them; after all, the people who are excited enough to think that they can change the world are the ones who do.

Two classes of outcomes

Along with the three levels, there are two classes of outcomes, both with very different levels of power. They are *standards* and *goals*.

This is one of the most powerful distinctions I made in my own life when it comes to psychology. It is something that, by itself, can put you at a huge advantage in the Unfair Fight, because it makes you draw from the depths of your power.

Essentially, you will live your standards, and maybe achieve your goals.

After my head injury I made the decision to raise the standards of my life. This was one of the most important decisions I ever made, because everything good in my life, everything in my life that I can be proud of, has come as a direct result of making that decision.

This sounds so simple, but don't discount it because of that. Raising your standards will change your life.

1. Goals

A goal is a target that you want to achieve, if it's convenient. Most people approach goals with the mindset of 'I'll achieve this if I can, but failure is okay.' They haven't truly decided, so they leave themselves a small out. This can lead to negative goal-setting and actually prevent them achieving what they want. This mindset is fine if the outcome isn't that important, such as picking up your dry-cleaning on a normal work day, but not when it's critical, such as picking up your dry-cleaning for your wedding day (which I learnt from experience!).

2. *Standards*

A standard is an outcome that you will achieve no matter what it takes. A standard involves a real decision, a real commitment; there is no 'out'. This is 100 per cent positive goal-setting. Standards have consequences, both in the form of massive pleasure when you achieve what you want and massive pain when you don't. When something's a standard, then in the end if you aren't there, it's not the end because defeat is not an option.

To illustrate what I mean, consider the difference in power and certainty between these two statements:

'I aim to not hit my children.'

'My children are the most important things in the world to me, I have their best interests at heart, and I will do whatever it takes to protect them from harm. I will die for them.'

That's the difference between a standard and a goal; one is weak and one is ultimate strength.

Most people live with goals; the successful ones live with standards.

It's okay to have goals as well as standards, but make the important things in your life your standards.

I have a goal to own a Lamborghini, but I don't have one yet. We do, however, have our dream home in the country, which was 25 times the cost of a Lamborghini. So it's not just about the money. The car is a goal I don't really care about. I know I'll get one at some point, and it'll be cool when I do, but it certainly doesn't impact on my life and my level of happiness. The house is a standard that means everything, because it's for my family.

Outcomes are an area where you have a massive advantage over your larger competition. Big corporations all set goals, but they have no one there whose life depends on achieving that goal, like your business does. So failure is an option, it's a 'write-off' on the balance sheet that will be 'washed up' in the end-of-year accounts.

The Unfair Fight is living with standards.

2. YOUR DRIVING FORCE: YOUR COMPELLING REASON 'WHY'

Once you know what you're aiming for, you have your target. Most people don't even get this far, but for those who do, this is where the majority stop. But that's like deciding to go on a trip and getting in a car that doesn't have a full tank of petrol. You are unlikely to get to your destination, especially if it's a long trip.

Most outcomes that will excite you won't come immediately. They are a long trip, so you need a lot of fuel to get there.

When you have the right amount of fuel, then almost nothing can stop you. If you are in a 5 000-kilometre race and you have unlimited fuel and your competition has half a tank of petrol, you can't lose – and that's just unfair!

Your fuel comes from answering the question: 'Why do I really want this?' Your answer moves the outcome from a 'should' to a 'must', from a goal to a standard, and you are tapping into your true power.

Most of us do more for others than we do for ourselves, so for your 'why' to be really powerful, you want to think about why it's important for the people you care about – your customers and your community – as well as why it's important for you.

In general, we all do more to avoid pain than to gain pleasure. Would you do more to protect the life of your child or to create a baby? Would you do more to protect the $1 million you have already made or to make it?

So make sure your 'why' not only covers what you'll gain from achieving the outcome, but also what it would cost you to not achieve the outcome. Be brutally honest, because this is what will set you up with the best fuel possible.

When I came out of my coma, I had a hard road ahead of me. Serious head injuries are unpredictable, with no guarantee of recovery, and the road to recovery is long and tortuous. I dealt with hurdles and setbacks hundreds of times a day, for many months. At the time, the recovery was the hardest challenge I had ever had to face, and there is no question that if I hadn't had a compelling reason 'why' recovery was so important, I would have given up.

If I hadn't had my compelling reason 'why', I might not have put up such a fight when the doctors tried to send me to a halfway house to recover; I might not have worked so hard to get back into shape physically; I might not have worked so hard to recover mentally; and I might not have had the strength of will to give up the alcohol I was abusing. Your 'why' is like your armour; you need it to be strong enough so that nothing can penetrate either it or your resolve.

When your external situation isn't giving you much certainty, you must create your own. I wanted more than anything to be able to think clearly again, to be able to function at a high level again, to be independent again, to feel energetic and joyful again, to go to medical school again, and to ski again. I also desperately didn't want to live with headaches, tiredness, low mood, muddled thinking and limited activity for the rest of my life.

The 'why' was so strong that I never gave up, not even after the 10 000th hurdle; recovery was a must and nothing was going to stop me getting back to my best.

If you're knocked over 1 000 times, then you'll get up 1 001 times if you have a strong enough 'why'. Without it, you might not get up enough times to get where you're aiming to be.

Against the odds, I came back much better than I ever was before. And I even got the greatest gift that I hadn't even realised I wanted in the form of meeting my wife-to-be; that's the power of the 'why'.

When the 'why' is strong enough, the 'how' will always reveal itself.

When you have a stronger 'why' than your competition, it's unfair, because you have much stronger fuel.

When you know what would truly excite you, and why you want it, then you are not fighting fair – because in my experience, less than 1 per cent of the population is clear on these two things.

3. BELIEF

'You do not become what you want, you become what you believe.'
– OPRAH WINFREY

In 1983, potato farmer Cliff Young decided to run the 875-kilometre Sydney to Melbourne ultra-marathon. He turned up dressed as a farmer, and people asked him if he'd run in races this length before. He told them that he hadn't, and when asked why he was starting with the longest race in Australia, he answered that it was the only race that fitted into his schedule.

While all the other runners had trained for years with the best coaches, had the right running equipment and had long-distance running experience, Cliff Young had a secret weapon – he'd never been trained by anyone, so he didn't know that you were supposed to sleep every 18 hours.

The runners set off, and immediately Cliff fell behind. He ran with a slow, loping pace for five-and-a-half days, and while the other runners slept every 18 hours, because that's what they had been taught to do, Cliff Young slept a lot less. Cliff Young finished the race first, taking two days off the record time.

Because no one had told Cliff that he couldn't do it, because he believed that he could run without sleeping every 18 hours, he did it. And he did it faster than anyone ever had before.

Sometimes what you think you know gets in the way of what's possible.

> 'Never tell a young person that anything cannot be done.
> God may have been waiting for centuries for someone
> ignorant enough of the impossible to do that very thing.'
>
> — G.M. TREVELYAN

A belief is a feeling of total certainty about the meaning of something. It is not necessarily based on a foundation of reality.

Beliefs act as filters to the world. They sift out the bits of reality that don't fit into your belief system, and allow you to become aware of the aspects of reality that are in alignment. They are incredibly powerful, because your beliefs determine what experiences you will have in life.

You form beliefs by focusing on selective facts of events that you perceive as real. If you perceived an event as a negative experience, you would then start to notice and attract similar experiences that would, in turn, reaffirm your beliefs about the situation. On the other hand, if you perceived the same event as a positive experience, then you might start to notice and attract similar positive experiences that reaffirm that belief.

Three beliefs that I have found critical to achieving anything great, to making any change, are:
1. This must change.
2. I must change it.
3. I can change it.

When something becomes a must, when you take total responsibility for making it happen, and when you believe that you can do it, then it's amazing what you can achieve.

There are two effective ways to change your beliefs to ensure that the ones that drive you, the ones that filter your perception of the world, are empowering beliefs:

1. References
Collect positive facts about any situation from your life or the lives of others to support new and more empowering ways of perceiving that situation. Always remember, if someone else can do it, so can you. The good in a situation is always there if you look for it, and so is the bad.

2. Affirmations
Spend five minutes a day for a minimum of 30 days affirming a new belief with positive incantations. This is covered in detail in the next step, 'Activate'.

> *'Whether you think you can, or you think you can't – you're right.'*
> — HENRY FORD

Belief is critical to achieving greatness, and you can instill belief using the steps below.

4. ACTIVATE
Once you know what you want, why you want it and you believe it is possible, then it's time to activate yourself in the direction of the outcome.

The universe is all energy, matter vibrating at different frequencies, and activation is about creating a vibrational match between you and what you desire.

Activation sets you up for success and mobilises all the resources available to you.

There are two key ways to doing this:

1. Incantations

You need to feel the feelings that will accompany your desired outcome as if it were real now. By doing this, your energy vibrates at the right frequency in order to attract the outcome into your life.

Incantations are done in the present tense, and the great ones describe the feeling that accompanies the outcome. Say them out loud, engage your body and emotions, and feel them as real now.

Some great affirmations that I enjoy are:

'I am revelling in my $3 million per year personal income.'

'I love the passion and fun between me and Claire every day that make her feel like a goddess.'

'I cherish the deep connection with my girls, which makes them feel loved and adored.'

'I thrill in my vibrant health and vitality.'

These all tell me how I feel and what to focus on, and they also reinforce, in the present tense, the standards I have chosen for my life. I feel great just saying the incantations and associating with them, and they focus me on what's important.

With incantations, remember the second commitment you made in Round 1: I am committed to action. Incantations without action are the beginning of delusion, while incantations with action are the beginning of miracles.

In the world of personal development, too many people see incantations as the outcome, whereas in reality they are just a tool to move you towards your outcome. They must be accompanied by massive action.

Say it. Be it. Do it.

2. Visualisation

It is incredibly powerful to visualise every day the important outcomes that you are striving for. The subconscious mind doesn't know the difference between what is real and what is vividly imagined, so visualisation turns the energy flow in the direction you want it to go.

You can do this as an eyes-closed exercise, or you can create a vision board with images of your standards.

Simply see what you want in your life as if it were already there. Make the images as vivid as possible, emotionally associate with them, feel the feelings you would feel as if you had what you want now. If you struggle with visualising images, that's okay; just feel the feelings. Remember that the language of the subconscious is both images and emotions, so use whichever one works best for you.

5. SUCCESS HABITS

If you want to get fit, you don't just go to the gym once, do a workout, then pat yourself on the back and say, 'Job done.' You need to exercise regularly over time and eat a healthy diet, and you need to do this for life, because the moment you stop, the decline starts.

Creating your success psychology is exactly the same. It's not about 'fixing' yourself, then never having to think about it again. It's about setting up habits that you practise daily for life.

When you begin, incantations and visualisation must be done for a minimum of 30 days straight. I have experienced time and again that it takes 25 to 30 days for the brain to create new neural pathways, for people to develop new beliefs, new habits, and to change their perceptions of the world.

Jack Canfield, in the same talk I mentioned earlier, shared an experiment NASA did with astronauts, making them wear glasses with concave lenses that flipped the image of the world upside down to see how they might react to zero gravity. Incredibly, after 25 to 30 days, all the astronauts' brains had flipped the inverted image and they perceived the world the right way up. Interestingly, for those astronauts who took the glasses off for a short time on Day 15, it took another 25 to 30 days before they experienced the correction by their brains.

You can't miss a single day – it's that important.

Small things done repeatedly over time lead to exceptional results.

So in reality the 30 days to form a habit is just the start. Commit 100 per cent to the 30 days, though, and my guess is that you'll be hooked, as you'll have gained momentum.

FANATICAL BALANCE

Balance is one of the most overrated things and has no part in the Unfair Fight. In my experience, most people who strive for 'balance' in their lives, people who make it a goal, usually live lives of mediocrity.

'Everything in moderation' is the mantra of the people who strive for balance. What about heroin in moderation, killing people in moderation, lying and cheating in moderation? It's a ridiculous thing to say or believe. For me, moderation equals mediocrity.

Balance can never be the goal in a life of excellence, but it can be the effect of a well-planned existence.

Rather than asking, 'How can I achieve balance in my life?', don't you think a better question is, 'How can I live an extraordinary life where I am making progress in all the areas that are important to me?'

Fanatical Balance is about prioritising what's important. And it is important in itself, because fulfilment is its direct result. And fulfilment gives you an exceptional life with the energy to persist.

The key to Fanatical Balance is to get clear about what's important to you in the following seven areas:

- Finance
- Business or career
- Fun
- Health and fitness

- Relationships
- Personal growth
- Contribution and purpose

By setting outcomes for what's important in each of these areas – what it would take to live a life of fulfilment – you give yourself a framework to make decisions in the future.

When you say 'Yes' to anything, you are saying 'No' to something else – fact. The key to a fulfilling existence is to make sure you are not saying 'Yes' to the unimportant at the expense of the important.

The reality is that anything you want in life is probably available to you, if you give something up. Where in your life are you saying 'Yes' to the unimportant – Facebook, TV, meaningless catch-ups, etcetera – at the cost of saying 'No' to what's really important to you? What's the true cost of wasted time?

For example, I am crystal clear on my objectives for my businesses, and I am crystal clear on my objectives for my family relationships. It is a must for me to get home in time to give my daughters their dinner and baths and to have a play with them before bed. This means leaving work at around 5.30 p.m., 6 p.m. at the latest. I am also very clear on what I want to achieve in my businesses on a daily, weekly, monthly, quarterly and yearly basis. Every morning I plan my day to achieve what I need to and also to be at home in time for my daughters. Therefore, I don't have general catch-ups with people, I don't meet many people for a coffee, and my meetings have an objective and they run to a schedule.

This might seem limiting, but in fact it is liberating, because I don't have to think too much about what I say 'Yes' to. I just decide if it will take me closer to my objectives, or not, and act accordingly. I don't miss out on precious time with my daughters or wife because I got sucked into a coffee with someone for no reason. And, as a result, my time is spent creating a life I want, rather than conforming to someone else's schedule.

Let's pretend for a while …

Imagine yourself in 10 years' time looking back on the past decade.

First imagine that you kept saying 'Yes' to the unimportant, to 'moderation'. You got your precious time on Facebook, you had lots of catch-ups with people and you kept a close eye on *Celebrity Big Brother*. But you missed all the important things in your life and, as a result, your life is like most people's – not where you want it to be. Your health isn't where you want it, you've put on a few pounds, your business is struggling and you haven't achieved financial freedom, and your relationship with your partner is flat.

Now imagine that you got clear on what was important and you developed a decision-making framework to say 'Yes' to what was important and 'No' to the unimportant. And, although your Facebook account is looking a bit lean, you didn't have as many cups of coffee and you have no idea who won *Celebrity Big Brother*, your business is flourishing and you have achieved financial freedom, you have a happy and passionate relationship with your partner, you are vibrant and healthy, you are making a positive contribution to a charity you've set up, and you've had a great time doing it.

Now which scenario sounds more appealing?

And was it a real cost to achieve the latter? Or just a perceived cost at the time?

Remember, successful people do what unsuccessful people aren't prepared to do. While this might seem like extra work, it's your choice, because ultimately *you* decide whether you live a life of fulfilment or not, a life of excellence or not. When your life is where you want it to be, balance becomes irrelevant, as all the important parts of your life get the appropriate attention.

Create excellence in what's important, not mediocrity in everything.

PERSIST, WORK HARD AND DON'T BE AFRAID TO FAIL

Don't be afraid to fail, but never fail because you didn't work hard enough.

The road to the top is always uphill. If you want to transcend your competition using the Unfair Fight, then be prepared to work for it; no one is going to drop success in your lap. Repetition is the mother of skill, so you'll have heard some of this before. But that's okay, because this point is so important. Muscles grow because you take them to their breaking point, then you push beyond that breaking point. That's how we grow, too. We go to our breaking point, then push beyond to where we have no choice but to grow or go home.

Failure is only failure if you let it be the end, but if you pick yourself up, learn from it and come back to fight another day, then it's just a temporary setback.

Challenge is inevitable, defeat is not.

If you get knocked down 1 000 times, how many times will you get up?

Something to always remember is that when you are partying or playing around, someone is working harder than you. They are getting smarter and getting ahead. Never forget this, and never forget that you can use this in your favour, too; when your competition is partying, you can be working harder than them, you can be getting smarter, you can be getting ahead.

The difference between winning and excellence is that winning is one time and excellence is continuous. The Unfair Fight is about creating excellence; it's not a one-time thing. Excellence is like exercising – you can't go to the gym once and think you're done; you've got to do it continuously. Everything you are learning here is not a one-time thing; mind bullets must be honed every day, so persist with them. Treat them just like a daily habit, such as brushing your teeth.

You'll then discover that success is a habit.

Don't be afraid to fail, but never fail because you didn't work hard enough.

GRATITUDE

Success in your business will help you get what you want, and happiness will come when you are grateful for what you have.

Your journey in the Unfair Fight will absolutely get you what you want in business. However, it's important not to think of where you are now as the 'wrong' place. Everything you have done and experienced in your life has got you to this moment, and this moment is right on time. Be grateful for where you are, and be excited about where you are going.

Most people live their lives in stress and anxiety and they forget to be grateful. In so doing, you are missing out on a massive power that will drive you and cause you to soar to great heights. Gratitude is key to positive goal-setting and to harnessing the power of your subconscious mind. Harnessing this power is part of the Unfair Fight, because those who live with gratitude put themselves at a massive advantage.

If you struggle to feel gratitude at the start, then just think about what you 'could' be grateful for. Keep doing this, and you will start to feel real gratitude.

As an entrepreneur I spend a lot of time focused on the future, on where I am taking my business. For a long time this meant that I didn't live in the present, I didn't celebrate the present, I wasn't grateful for the present – I was always focused on the next outcome.

When I learnt to keep an eye on the future but to live in the present and be grateful for it, life became much better and I became a lot happier.

'Walk as if you are kissing the earth with your feet.'
— THÍCH NHÂT HANH

And the cool thing is that this gave me more energy to create a compelling future.

MAKING IT REAL

Successful people do what unsuccessful people aren't prepared to do. This is going to take some time, but it should be a lot of fun, and it only takes five to 15 minutes each day to get you on track for the day and on track in your life. Isn't that a worthwhile investment?

Below I've outlined a simple process you can follow to make this real for you, to hone your mind bullets. Each step and the order each step is in is important, so please don't skip anything. You will astound yourself with the impact this can have on your life, and your business.

Exercise
1. Clarity
a. Get clear on what's important to you. For each core category, answer the question 'What would excite me?'
  • Relationships
  • Business or career
  • Health and fitness
  • Personal growth
  • Finance
  • Fun
  • Contribution and purpose
b. Decide on one to three standards for each category.

2. Driving force
a. For each standard, record why it is a must for you to achieve it.

Record what you'll gain by achieving it, and what you'll lose if you don't.

3. Belief and activation

a. Create an incantation to support each category. Ensure that it covers how you wish to feel and what your standard is.

4. Take massive action and make it real

a. Protect those standards by consciously choosing what you say 'Yes' to – be like a mother bear protecting her cubs.

b. Create success habits that you do every day to drive your ongoing success. Start with a Daily Morning Ritual that will direct the tide of your subconscious mind and will set you up for success. It will also get you feeling great about your day and your life:

- Get into a state of gratitude. Start with yourself and move out in ever-widening circles of gratitude: self, family, friends, business, your community, your country, God, etcetera – whatever is important to you.
- Review each of your categories – your standards and your driving forces.
- Say your incantations out loud.
- Visualise either using an eyes-closed exercise or by reviewing your vision board.
- Write down your standards and plan your day.
- Do this daily for a minimum of 30 days (and I bet you'll keep doing it, because it's so powerful).

To really crank this up and to create massive results in your life, you can access the Life Creation Tool by registering at www.samhazledine.com.

Have fun. This exercise is about creating an exceptional life on your terms, a life you love, a life you can be proud of.

It will start the process of setting you up for success, but the key to ensuring success is what you do daily. Excellence is a process; it's not a one-off.

SUMMARY

In essence, this section is ultimately about the difference between mastery and dabbling. Most people spend their lives dabbling, trying out new things and changing direction, never really mastering anything or creating excellence.

People who achieve greatness commit to mastery. Mastery is like laying down building blocks – to build a skyscraper, you have to do it systematically and you have to do each stage well, or your building will fall down. Life is like this too. If you dabble and throw your building blocks down erratically, you'll never get very high and you will keep falling over. However, if you commit to mastery and build the layers of your life well, then you, too, can reach the sky.

Mastery is a habit; great things are achieved by doing the small things well and by doing them repeatedly. Your habits are defining your life, so make sure that you consciously choose habits that support you.

Mastery takes self-discipline. You have to stick at it. This entire chapter has given you the tools to create mastery in your life – you just need to commit to it.

It really is that simple.

Start with 30 days and I bet you'll be hooked, because the results will speak for themselves.

Many great books have been written on the subject of mindset and I don't think it has to be particularly complicated; life mastery is simply a matter of consistently doing what you need to do to make sure your subconscious mind is moving in the same direction as your conscious mind wants to. Then your life moves in that direction, too.

This can be achieved by focusing on what you want and why you want it, by creating a life of fulfilment where you make progress in all the important areas, by persisting and never giving up, and by ultimately being grateful for where you are and where you are going.

I don't know you personally yet, but I feel that we are on a journey together because you are reading this book. You want more, and I know your life will be blessed if you just allow it to be.

Because you are mastering yourself first, you are putting yourself in that sweet spot where a peak mindset and directed actions can meet, which is exactly where you need to be to create an exceptional business.

Harness a power that is available to you right now; choose to become a master of the principles in this book. You will transcend the competition and start living the Unfair Fight.

ROUND 4

Leadership

In business, if you are stepping into the ring alone, you are already facing unfair odds. Therefore, a cornerstone of the Unfair Fight is to effectively mobilise your people, and one critical way to do this is through effective leadership.

Are great leaders born or made?

What I've learnt by observing hundreds of people in business is that, like most things, the capability for leadership falls along a bell curve. Some people are certainly born leaders. These people start out at the top of the bell curve and just get better as they go along. Then there are those people at the bottom of the curve, the 10 to 15 per cent who, no matter how hard they try, are going to struggle to be great leaders. Then there's the middle of the curve, where the majority of us live. This is where you'll find the real potential for 'made' leaders. Most people who start out with even a modicum of innate leadership ability can actually become great leaders when they know how.

Leadership is the ability to align people behind a vision, to allow them to see an opportunity in their world and willingly take action to move towards a common outcome. Top talent leaves organisations when they're badly managed and the organisation is confusing and uninspiring – essentially when there is ineffective leadership.

This is an area that is critical to master if you want to effectively apply the Unfair Fight and move beyond competing, to excelling, in business.

Given that you have read this far, I am assuming that you have the potential to be a great leader, or that you might already be one. This chapter will give you the 12 learnable traits and practices to become a great leader.

12 CHARACTER TRAITS AND SKILLS OF GREAT LEADERS
1. They have integrity and authenticity

The foundation of great leadership is integrity. This is the integration of outward actions and inner values; great leaders are the same on the outside as they are on the inside. A great leader is authentic. Values guide decisions and, while a leader needs to be like a river, flexible and able to adapt to the environment, their values must stay solid, like a rock in the river.

An authentic leader understands that for their business to achieve success, they must first become the leader who deserves that success, and who deserves to attract the people who will create that success for the business.

Being authentic isn't complicated, but it can be challenging. Here are the behaviours you can practise daily that build integrity:

- Do the right thing, always.
- Do what you say you're going to do.
- Be honest in your conversations, even if the truth is uncomfortable.
- Only make promises that you can keep.
- Be willing to deal quickly with those in your team who act without integrity.

- Be loyal to the company, its visions, values and goals, and have the backs of your team.
- Don't let others sway you away from acting with integrity, whatever their position.

2. They have vision

The vision for a company sets the focus. How to create a great vision is covered in Round 2 (see page 64). It is something that captures the 'why' of the business, it lifts people up and it inspires them to excellence.

A great leader not only creates a compelling vision, but also communicates that vision in a way their people can understand and get behind:

- Learn to paint a picture with words – make the vision compelling.
- Make sure your employees can tell you, in their own words, what they think the vision for the company is. Is their interpretation the same as yours?

Your company's vision should be in the minds of you and your team every day.

You should re-evaluate your vision periodically so that it stays current with the changing environment. Your team needs to be just as involved as you in keeping it up to date if you truly want them to buy into the vision.

Great leaders also have another kind of vision – the ability to see around corners, to anticipate the radically unexpected. In reality no one is born with a sixth sense that can predict what will happen in the market. It takes time to get a feel for what your customers will want in the future, it takes time to get a feel for what your competitors are thinking and to be able to predict their next moves. But the bottom line is the sooner you can develop and hone this skill, the better placed you will be as a leader of your company.

3. They are passionate

Your team wants passion; in fact, people will go to the ends of the earth because of it. People will live and die for it, such is the desire for passion in our lives. Think of the soldiers who travelled with Hernán Cortés to conquer the Aztec empire, heading into the unknown, not knowing if they would ever return. Their leader's passion, his belief in what they could achieve in the face of adversity, inspired them to put their very lives at risk.

To build an extraordinary team, you've got to light the 'fire in their bellies', so they feel passion for the company and connect with the vision. Passion is such a key part of being a great leader that if you don't have it, you simply can't be a great leader – if *you* don't have it, you can't expect your team to have it.

Passion is infectious. When you talk about your vision for the company and your team, let your passion for your vision shine through. Others will feel it and want to get on board with you. If you don't have passion for your vision, you need to recreate your vision or reframe your description of your vision so it's connected to your passion. It's that important.

When I started MedRecruit I had no business experience, but I had huge amounts of passion: passion to improve the lives of doctors, passion to assist hospitals with their staffing, and passion to create a great company. Because this passion was genuine, and because people knew it was genuine, they gave me a chance. They said 'Yes' to doing business with a recruitment company with no doctors! But without the passion I would have been just another person trying to make a buck and we wouldn't have made it out of the starting gates. Passion was the difference.

4. They are bold

Nice leaders are liked by everyone, but they don't have the courage to say what needs to be said. They are therefore weak and are walkovers.

Fierce leaders don't think of other people's feelings and they use force to get their way. They aren't liked and, as soon as their backs are turned, people will undermine them.

Bold leaders have both compassion and courage. They listen to people and are sensitive to their situation and their needs, and they are courageous enough to say what needs to be said and do what needs to be done. Nothing changes until the unsaid is spoken. The truth will set you free, and bold leaders understand this and apply it.

5. They set the focus

Where focus goes, energy flows. Your team will focus wherever you are focusing, so a great leader consciously decides where to focus, and hence where the team needs to focus.

The importance of focus is to get people to take actions that move them towards their objectives and the company's objectives. Therefore, you need to make sure that they are clear on both their personal objectives and the company's objectives, and also the Critical Drivers, which are the actions they must take personally to succeed in their role. More on Critical Drivers in Round 8.

Effective focus will take people from being task-driven to being outcome-driven, and will accelerate their progress towards achieving your company's goals.

Early on in my business I was excited about everything and I kept focusing on new opportunities. I soon learnt that this confused my team, because they couldn't predict where I'd be putting my energy next and they didn't know what was important. There was a lot of two steps forward, one step back, one step to the side, then back, then forward again! First I had to get clear on what was important, then I could put my focus there, and then my team knew where to focus. As a result we became a lot more effective and a lot more successful.

6. They are great team builders

The success of a great leader is not an accident, and most leaders would agree it's not a testament to their ability alone. They consistently surround themselves with talented people and build that talent into a great team. They are not afraid of hiring people who are better than them; in fact, they welcome it, because they know it's critical to achieving progress.

They also recognise that there are too many moving parts to control single-handedly, so they concentrate on what they do best and delegate appropriately. Importantly, they delegate to people who have demonstrated competence in the task required.

7. They set the standard and demand accountability

Great leaders set a standard of excellence for all tasks in an organisation.

> *'Shined shoes save lives.'*
> — GENERAL NORMAN SCHWARZKOPF

Great leaders understand that exceptions are the enemies of excellence and that tolerance of slipshod is the start of the slippery slope to decline.

Great leaders will instil a culture of accountability in their organisation. They ensure that people come to them with proposals and solutions, not just problems.

One method I have found to be very effective is to never let a team member just come to me with a problem they want me to solve. That is just making their problem my problem. I ensure that they also bring me three possible solutions and their recommendation on how best to proceed. Do this enough and soon people will start to figure things out for themselves. And in turn this will empower them to be their best.

8. They are creative and open

Creativity is the ability to think differently, to get outside of the box that constrains solutions, and to come up with new ways of looking at and solving problems.

Great leaders have the ability to see things that others have not seen, and so they can lead followers in new directions. Three of the most important questions that a leader can ask are: 'What if?', 'What more can we do?' and 'How else could that work?'

Great leaders are open to new ideas, even if these ideas don't conform to the norm, or if they come from other people. They will suspend judgement while listening to new ideas and will welcome ideas that aren't their own.

The leader who thinks that he has to come up with all the good ideas is severely limiting his business. By being open, you will also build mutual respect and trust with your employees, which fuels your team to continue to come up with new and better ideas to further the company's vision.

9. They are great decision-makers

Great leaders make decisions quickly and are committed to those solutions. This means that they stick with their decisions, because they are not swayed by common opinion, which often flies in the face of the best course of action. But great leaders are not so rigid that they will never change their mind.

They are analytical in that they will make decisions based on the facts at hand, but they won't over-analyse and paralyse themselves.

They will be thoughtful to all parties concerned, but they will understand that they can't please everyone, and, in fact, that is not their goal.

10. They are magnanimous

Great leaders give credit where it is due. A magnanimous leader ensures that credit for successes is spread as widely as possible throughout the company. Conversely, a good leader will take personal responsibility for failures. This sort of reverse magnanimity helps other people feel good about themselves, draws the team closer together, and encourages both respect and trust for their leader.

To 'spread the fame and take the blame' is a hallmark of great leaders. They aren't looking for the credit, they are looking for results.

They acknowledge people and say thank you.

11. They are engaged and present in their surroundings

Great leaders are present and engaged in the moment. They value their time and they respect other people's time too. They ensure that there is structure to meetings and that discussions stay on track. A great leader will give the situation their complete attention – you won't find them texting while they talk to you.

12. They are positive

As noted by digital-marketing expert Damian Bazadona in his Inc. com article '6 Traits of Great Leaders', passionate leaders are inherently optimistic. They genuinely believe that anything is possible and want to be surrounded by people who are enthusiastic and keep them inspired.

Great leaders are likely to be openly frustrated when there is a roadblock or a wave of negativity, because they see this as a hindrance towards achieving great things. They have no time for pessimism; failure is not an acceptable answer.

A great leader believes that, in the end, if you haven't achieved what you need to achieve, it's not the end.

OUTCOME: TRUST

The result of these 12 character traits and skills is that they build trust. Trust is gained by delivering consistently over time and is essential to aligning people towards a common outcome. Without trust, people won't buy 100 per cent into a leader; they will always hold something back. When people totally trust their leader, they will follow them into the unknown, which is where leaders need to go to forge new ground.

The key dimensions that underpin trust for leaders in a business are:

- **Integrity** – honesty and truthfulness. Doing the right thing, even if it's the thing that takes the most effort. And it means doing it even if no one were to know about it.
- **Competence** – encompasses a leader's technical and interpersonal knowledge and skills. People need to believe that their leader has the skills to carry out what she says she will.
- **Consistency** – relates to a leader's reliability, predictability and good judgement in handling situations. Inconsistencies between words and actions decrease trust.
- **Loyalty** – the willingness to save face for another person. Trust requires that you can depend on someone not to act opportunistically.
- **Openness** – can you tell the whole truth? It is important for leaders to be transparent.

Leadership comes at a cost. The trust you gain as a leader is dependent on you continuing to work harder to look after others rather than you working to look after yourself. Trust requires that you sacrifice yourself in some way for the benefit of others.

Ensure that your actions make you a trusted leader who deserves the respect of your team, and your effectiveness in business will be increased exponentially.

Do the following exercise to learn the 12 character traits and skills of a great leader.

Exercise

1. Focus on one of these character traits or skills each week for the next 12 weeks.
2. Review the notes on that trait or skill three times a day – once when you wake, once at lunchtime, and once before you go to bed.
3. Focus on that trait or skill throughout the day and actively live it.
4. Ensure that every week you master the trait and skill you are focusing on.

At the end of the 12 weeks you will embody the traits and skills of a great leader.

THRIVING AS A LEADER THROUGH TOUGH TIMES

Problems are a fact of life, and they're a fact of business. When the market is going well, you have challenges, and when the market is going badly, you have challenges.

The world is going through change at such a fast rate that there are always going to be challenges. As we get better at business we don't get rid of problems, we just create better-quality problems. Therefore, as a leader it's important to know how to thrive not only in the good times, but also in the tough times.

If you are currently experiencing tough times in your business, then think about how you've been showing up in your business, and learn what you need to from this next section to make your business thrive again.

Beliefs

Thriving as a leader in tough times starts with you, the leader. It starts with your beliefs.

As the leader you must adopt the belief that anything less than the best isn't tolerated, because if you don't, if you give up and start compromising, then it's a slippery slope.

For a leader to thrive in tough times, in any times, you must adopt these three beliefs:

1. It must change.
Leaders make the need for change non-negotiable.

2. I must change it.
Leaders take total responsibility for making the change happen.

3. I can change it.
Leaders believe that they, along with their resources, can achieve the necessary change.

Tolerating the problem is not in the DNA of a great leader.

The four steps to thrive in tough times

1. Embrace
Tough times breed great leaders. Abraham Lincoln wouldn't be heralded as a great leader if he hadn't faced up to slavery and taken it upon himself to right that terrible wrong.

Great leaders understand that tough times give them the chance to rewrite the book, so they get excited about challenges. Only dead fish swim with the current. Great leaders swim against the current and use these times to come up with great ideas that help them survive, and then thrive, when things inevitably improve.

So the first thing to do is to be open to the problem and welcome it as a necessary step towards your ultimate outcome.

2. Pause and ponder

When times get tough, most people's flight-or-fight response kicks in and they panic. Reaction is rarely the best response, so it's important that you pause and ponder if you want to thrive in tough times.

The first thing to do is to determine what the real problem is, not the symptom that presents as the 'squeaky wheel'. To do this, you need to keep asking, 'So what's *really* the problem?' as you dive deeper, until you cannot go any deeper. Get to the root problem, and then you can find a solution that will really work.

Confront reality and use analytics where possible. During tough times you don't want to be making things up; you need all your wits about you to survive.

Effective thinking requires a conscious effort – it requires you to pause, to remove yourself from the 'noise', and to determine what's really happening.

3. Engage

In tough times you need to engage with your people. This is important both to get better ideas and to ensure that your team is on board with whatever solution is found.

- Be transparent when you present the problem to your team.
- Get agreement that it's a real problem.
- Get agreement that it needs to be solved (make it intolerable).
- Don't panic.

Encourage your team to come up with ideas to both solve the problem to get you back to the status quo, and to capitalise on the problem to evolve the status quo.

Engage with the resistors, the people who aren't 100 per cent on board. It's amazing what you can learn from them. When you engage with them and they feel heard, they can become your biggest advocates, which has the effect of massively lifting your entire team.

4. *Act*

Sitting around thinking and talking isn't going to do anything to help you thrive in tough times unless you take action.

Be bold, be decisive. This is not a time to tread hesitantly.

Build the machine to solve the problem, taking into account both the short and long term.

Remember, you don't have to do it alone, but it's the leader's job to take ownership and to stay engaged with monitoring and measuring success.

> *'Leadership is lifting a person's vision to higher sights,*
> *the raising of a person's performance to a higher standard,*
> *the building of a personality beyond its normal limitations.'*
> — PETER DRUCKER

Use the tough times to upgrade your business and your people. Step up and bring your people with you.

To minimise crises and tough times it's important to engage in
'No Surprises Leadership'. To obtain an unpublished chapter on
No Surprises Leadership, register at www.samhazledine.com.

SUMMARY

Becoming a great leader is critical to your business success; you can't achieve what you need to on your own. Leadership is not a rank, it's a decision you make to take care of other people, to create a safe environment for them to be their best. Make the decision to master leadership and to become the leader you must be to deserve the level of success you want, whether times are good or bad, and to attract the people you need.

By doing this you won't be getting into the ring alone, you'll be getting in with a team, an aligned team, an effective team.

You'll have the power of a team of people working as a unit fighting a single person.

That's not fair.

That's the Unfair Fight.

PART 2

The Fight

Given you have read this far, you have decided to be successful, you've started the process of honing your mind bullets, you are getting yourself operating at your best, and you are becoming the leader your business needs. Congratulations! Just by getting yourself to this point, you have put yourself in the few who *do* versus the many who *talk*.

Now it's time to jump into the fight. You can't win standing on the sidelines.

Part 2 is dedicated to the 'how to', the actions you need to take to move beyond competing head to head. These actions will capitalise on the advantages you have over any large corporate, so that ultimately *you* win in business.

Personally I have found that most business books make this step complicated and confusing, but I don't think it needs to be that hard. I've put together the following chapters by taking the best ideas from multiple industries, the best lessons from the best teachers over the years, and from my own personal experience. The content in these chapters has been formed in the trenches of real business, not at a university, so they are in a simple-to-understand format with action steps for you to take.

Do the work and you will get the results.

This is a how-to manual that, when applied, will deliver massive success for your business.

Most people aren't prepared to do the work it takes to succeed in business; they are always looking for the silver bullet – a get-rich-quick scheme. There is no silver bullet, but there are some focused actions you can take to create exceptional results.

Because you have been through Part 1, you will be totally ready to implement what you learn in Part 2. Implementation of the ideas will be the difference between those who have an enjoyable read and those who create exceptional businesses.

What do *you* want?

ROUND 5

Differentiation

People in business are constantly talking about 'differentiating' their business, but what they generally understand this to mean is making their business 'different'. So business owners concentrate on how they can make their business stand out from the crowd.

This might or might not be a good idea and might grow or kill your business.

The Unfair Fight is not about making your business 'different' for the sake of it; it's about *defining* your business in the eyes of your customers as their only logical choice. It's about adding relevant value as well as making you different from your competition.

You've got to be better, as well as different.

RELEVANT DIFFERENTIATION

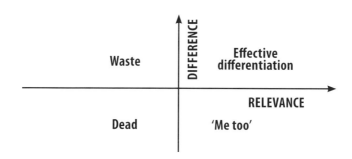

Ultimately in business, you want to be both relevant and different. This is where you not only differentiate yourself from your competition, but you appeal to what the customers want and make yourself the best choice.

DEAD

When you are neither different nor relevant, you are on your way out of business. You can tell if your business is in this category if your sales are struggling, you look like your competitors and your customers are ambivalent towards your product.

Action: If this is you, then you need to determine what value looks like to your customers, determine what your competitors are providing and find the gap in the market that you can fill. You need to pay very close attention to this chapter; the life of your business depends on it.

WASTE

Waste is when you have made great efforts to look different, to 'stand out' from the crowd, but you don't appeal to your customers. This is where many entrepreneurs take their businesses after attending a rocking business seminar, where 'differentiation' is the greatest word in the world, and where every wacky idea gets a high-five and an 'Atta boy!' You can tell if your business is in this category if you look different from your competitors but your sales are struggling, or if you get customers in the door but fail to get much repeat business.

Action: If this is you, then you need to follow the same instructions as if your business is Dead, because that's where it's heading.

'ME TOO'

This is when you provide something that your customers want, but you look just like everyone else providing it. You can tell if your business is in this category if your customers like you, you get some repeat business, but your business isn't growing steadily and it's hard to tell the difference between you and everyone else in your industry.

Action: This is the category where most companies that don't go out of business quickly end up – it's the area of mediocrity. If this is you, then you need to find the gap in the market, the space between what your customers want and what everyone is delivering, and fill that space.

EFFECTIVE DIFFERENTIATION

You are not only different from your competition, but you are also extremely relevant to your customers and provide them with exactly what they want and need. You can tell if you are in this category if your business is growing, you clearly look and are different from your competition, and your customers are extremely loyal. They wouldn't go anywhere else, and they come back again and again.

Action: If this is you, then it's important to continue to monitor the needs of your customers, ensuring that you keep providing them with what they want and keep solving their problems. Look closely at your competitors to make sure your point of difference is still different, and innovate to stay ahead of them. The danger in this category is that if you don't continue to innovate, then you will fall into the 'Me Too' category, because your competitors are looking at what you're doing and they will copy you.

When I started MedRecruit, I saw a gap in the market that was crying out to be filled – offering lifestyle for doctors. We launched the company with this as our Unique Client Advantage: 'Life and career, now you can have it all.' It was a great success and we grew very quickly. We were speaking the doctors' language, so they were naturally drawn to us.

However, it was so successful that I kept using it as our point of difference for too long. After a few years I realised that every other agency was talking about life and career, and what had started for us as Effective Differentiation was now 'Me Too'. Far from making us stand out from our competition, it was making us blend in.

The great thing is we helped to change the status quo of our industry to make lifestyle a valid ideal for doctors to aspire to. But once the status quo had changed, we had to go back to the market, find the new pain points, then evolve the company to be effectively different once again.

The competition you need to care about is likely to be in the 'Me Too' category and the Effective Differentiation category. If they are Dead or Waste, don't worry about them – let them go out of business without your help! The key to Effective Differentiation lies in understanding the needs of your market, understanding the problems your customers are facing, innovating to meet and exceed those needs, to solve those problems, and then positioning yourself effectively.

A great teacher of mine, Keith Cunningham, once said to me: 'Find out what they want, go out and get it, and give it to them.' This is the essence of Effective Differentiation. It's not rocket science, so don't make it harder than it needs to be.

Difference is pretty easy to see, but what most business owners don't know, and what none of the books will tell you in an effective and simple way, is how to determine exactly what is relevant to your customers and in your business.

This can be a complicated process, or it can be very simple. Complicated is hard to implement, simple is easy.

The Unfair Fight is simple, to the point and easy to implement.

There are two ways for you to increase your profits – either increase your revenue or decrease your expenses.

Effective Differentiation is about increasing your revenue, and it relies on three things: Benefit, Process and Source.

You can access the Differentiation to Profit Map and map your business by registering at www.samhazledine.com.

Most businesses will have more than one way of differentiating themselves, and to some extent most use all three ways; however, great businesses generally have one main way of differentiating because they know what's important to their customers, and they know what they want to stand for.

As you read this next section, think about:
- How you are currently differentiating your business.
- How you need to differentiate your business.

How you decide to differentiate your business is a choice, and your market and what your market is calling for both influence that choice.

While there are three broad ways to differentiate your business, and you might aspire to all three of them, it is important to choose a primary differentiation method so you can focus your time, energy and resources in one area to gain critical mass. Focusing on all three is likely to dissipate your effectiveness and you'll end up as 'nothing to nobody', rather than making your business stand out to your target market in a powerful way.

1. CREATE A NEW CATEGORY

Creating a new category is both the most challenging, and probably the most powerful, method to differentiate your business. This method is not for the faint-hearted, because essentially you are aiming to change the status quo of how people live.

Before Red Bull, there was no 'energy drink' category; they created the entire category and now, when you think 'energy drink', you think Red Bull plus a whole lot of imitators.

The creation of a new category is not primarily driven by resources, so it's an area where the small business owner can stand up and slay giants. The small business owner has an advantage here because, generally, the large corporates have so much momentum in one direction that creating a new category for them would be like trying to manoeuvre a super-tanker down a raging river.

How to create a new category

There isn't a simple prescribed formula to create a new category; changing the world isn't a 'paint-by-numbers' exercise, but there are principles that can be applied to increase your chances of success with this strategy.

1. Get clear on the status quo

To change the status quo, you need to be acutely aware of the current status quo, the current norm, the way people live. How is business done in your industry? What are the common choices people are making? What do people settle for?

2. Determine what they don't know they need

There are two types of evolution: gradual and sudden. Creating a new category is about sudden evolution.

While much of business success is about finding out what people want, then delivering it in the way they want it, changing a category is about determining what people don't yet know they need.

The current status quo is the box in which people's needs are currently met. Changing the status quo is either about meeting an as-yet unknown need, or meeting a number of known needs in a new coherent way; it's about finding out people's unmet aspirations.

Before smartphones, we had no idea that we needed a phone, a camera, email, weather updates, a clock, a calculator, directions, etcetera, in our pocket. We had all these needs, but smartphones developed to meet the group of needs in a unique and coherent way.

Before Red Bull, when people needed a pick-me-up, coffee would do the trick. They didn't realise that they wanted a boost in a way that made them feel like an extreme athlete, but they do now.

3. Deliver on the need in a new way

To create a new category, you have to think differently. By definition, the status quo is inside the current box; the creation of a new category is outside that box. Some great ways that I find help me to think outside the box are:

1. Study another industry: It's amazing how, when you look at how people solve problems in other industries, it opens up new ways of thinking about how to solve the problems in your industry.
2. Learn about something completely unrelated: Steve Jobs made this concept famous – in learning about things unrelated to the computer industry, he sparked new ways of looking at computers that created an entirely new category. As he said, 'If I had never dropped in on that single calligraphy course in

college, the Mac would have never had multiple typefaces or proportionally spaced fonts.'

3. Draw a picture: Drawing a picture is a really right-brained exercise that can help you break your logical left brain's position on how to solve a problem.

4. Ask a child for advice: Children have a certain ignorance that means they aren't constrained by the status quo, because they don't know what it is. Ask a child how they might tackle a problem, and then listen to what they are really saying. While creating a castle in the sky might not be your best way of differentiating your business, it might push you into thinking about how you might create a differentiation strategy that is just as unique.

4. Create a strong brand to define the category

Every 'category changer' must support their differentiation strategy with a powerful brand. This is a way to define the new category and link it to your company in the minds of the consumer.

People still Hoover the house, Xerox documents and put a Band-Aid over a cut, whether they are using these brands or not. All these companies not only created new categories, they supported them with strong brands.

5. Continue to redefine the category

Nothing stands still. Just because you have created a new category doesn't mean that a competitor can't out-differentiate you, using one of the other methods of effective differentiation.

2. BECOME THE AUTHORITY IN YOUR CATEGORY

People trust experts. You are infinitely more likely to trust a medical diagnosis from a doctor than an accountant, aren't you? By differentiating your company, by becoming the authority, you are choosing to build trust and therefore give people certainty of getting what they want by using you.

Becoming the authority is just as achievable for the small business owner as it is for the larger corporate, but the small business owner has an advantage, as they didn't come with all the preconceived perceptions from the market that corporates do.

How to become the authority – educate the market to own the market

There is a lot of talk in the marketing world that if you want to be seen as the expert, you just say you *are* the expert. I don't completely agree with this notion.

The key to being perceived as the expert, as the authority, is to deliver powerful information to the market. To ensure that you are seen as the authority, this information needs five hallmarks:

1. Is it unique?

Just delivering information that people can get elsewhere doesn't help position you as the authority. What you deliver to them must be unique; it must be something that makes them take notice.

2. Is it interesting?

Just being unique isn't enough; it must also be interesting to the target market. If you are a business owner and I was to share information about how to get your whites whiter and colours brighter in your washing, it probably wouldn't interest you. But if I shared information on how you can effectively differentiate your business to create ongoing success and, ultimately, make more money, you'd probably take notice.

3. Is it useful?

If I told you that in an average lifetime a person walks the equivalent of five times around the equator, you might be interested in that fact, but, because it's of no use to your business, it wouldn't help position me as the authority. To be seen as the authority, it's important to deliver information that can be used to create tangible benefits with your target market.

4. Is it within the area you have permission to be an expert in?

I love personal development, so at my medical recruitment company, MedRecruit, I shared a lot of information on goal achievement and mindset in our marketing. I thought this information was unique, interesting and useful, but it wasn't within the area that I was given permission to be the expert in by our target market. As such it didn't help business and, at times, it even harmed it. When we started delivering information about the supply and demand of jobs, and where doctors could earn the most money, we started to be perceived as the authority.

5. Are you delivering the information in a way people can easily understand the benefits?

Most people digest information thinking, 'What's in it for me?' To be seen as the authority, you have to deliver the information so that people can answer this question simply and easily.

If you educate the market with information that is unique, interesting, useful, in an area you have permission to be the expert in, and in a way that they can easily see the benefits, then you will be seen as the authority, because the one who educates the market, owns the market. When you own the market, you are effectively differentiated as the leader.

3. BE THE BEST IN YOUR CATEGORY

This is what most business owners fall back on to differentiate their business. This doesn't make it wrong, but it does mean that you need to be exceptionally good to use it to differentiate effectively.

The key here is being the best in what's important, and not just in the 'hygiene' factors in your industry; 'best service' is not differentiation.

How to become the best
Service businesses

The best area for most service-based businesses to differentiate is in the experience they provide to their customers. Any business can make their experience good, but good is not good enough; it needs to be so good that the customers can't help but talk about it; it needs to be breathtaking.

Here are the keys to creating a breathtaking experience:

1. Understand what the customer really wants

This is where it all starts. The key is to get into conversation with your customers and actually ask them what they want. This isn't complicated, but it's incredible how many business owners don't get clear on this first.

I was recently working with a business owner whose business removes rubbish. He had built a great business with a real focus on clean uniforms and trucks and great service. All the customers liked this, but when he got in front of them, they told him that the most important thing was speed; when you have rubbish, you want it gone yesterday. By understanding this, we could build a breathtaking experience that delivered what was really important.

2. Get the basics right

The bells and whistles are great, but if you don't get the basics right, then you're dead in the water. In my recruitment business it starts with getting the doctors the best-matched job, then taking care of all the details so that they start on time with minimum hassle. Getting them picked up in limousines, sending them gifts, the personal concierge service, etcetera would be of no use if we didn't get the basics right. You can't put icing on dog shit and call it cake; it might look nice but, as soon as people dig in, you're both in trouble.

3. Never treat a potential customer better than you treat a current customer

How do you feel when a company you have done business with for a long time offers new customers a better deal than you are getting? Most businesses get this horribly wrong because they focus on getting new customers and forget about their existing customers. Just get this bit right and you are going a long way to differentiating your business.

4. Make it easy and pleasant to do business with you

Identify any roadblocks that a customer might have in doing business with you, then remove them – it's that simple. You must make it very easy for people to make contact and do business with you. You also need to make it pleasant. This can be so easy: do simple things such as being enthusiastic on the phone and making sure the customer feels valued. Never make the customer feel like an interruption. Don't use phrases like 'TGIF' and 'I can't wait to finish my shift', because customers just hear that as 'You're getting in the way of me having a good day. Get out of my face.'

5. Deliver on your promises

Never over-promise, always over-deliver. Full stop.

6. Go above and beyond – 'wow' them

Once you have the basics right, it's time to blow them away. Look for opportunities to take their breath away with the unexpected.

7. Make your customers successful – guarantee their success

Make sure you know exactly what success looks like for your customers. Sometimes it's not what you think it is, so do some research with them. It might be making them look like a rock star in front of their boss, helping them connect with their family, helping them feel confident in their job … the key is to find out what it is, then deliver it.

Most businesses get it wrong because they focus on customer service, not customer satisfaction; customer service is about you – customer satisfaction is about them.

Do this and you'll make your customers so happy, they have no reason to go elsewhere.

Product businesses

When you have a product to sell, you can certainly differentiate with it. This is when you get into the race of being better, faster, cheaper, etcetera .

Here are four core ways to differentiate your product:

1. Quality

Be the best. You need to know what 'best' means from the perspective of your customers.

2. Price

Be the cheapest. This is a challenging space to be in, because there is always someone looking to undercut you.

3. Innovative functional features or design

Make your product the most effective at solving the customers' problems, or make it look the most appealing, so people just 'have to have it'.

If you are differentiating on innovation or on factors other than just price, then there are two core processes that are important to follow:

1. Continue to clarify the customer challenges: This is an ongoing conversation; you need to be crystal clear on the challenge that your customer is trying to overcome with your product. To focus yourself in the most effective direction, keep asking the question: 'How can I make my customers' lives easier, simpler and better?' The needs of your customers are constantly evolving, so make sure that you stay abreast of those changes and that your innovations are relevant.

2. Build it simple to solve the challenge: Good trumps trendy. Make sure that your innovations are based on better solving the customers' challenges, and not just making it cooler. Perfection is when there is nothing left to take away; focusing on what's important is your goal, not minimisation for the sake of it.

4. Availability – timing or location

Be the most effective at having your product in the right place at the right time, just when the customer needs it. If you're selling cold water, then you are infinitely more likely to sell it if you are in a place where people are thirsty, with limited access to it.

If you are differentiating your business by your product, then you need to make sure that your customers see your product as not only unique, but also relevant to what they want. As long as you follow this rule, your product will be seen as different and better and it will develop its own niche. It becomes harder and harder to categorise and hence draws fewer comparisons with its competition.

A successful product-differentiation strategy will move your product from competing on price to competing on other factors, and the more successful you become, the more you own your space and make the competition irrelevant.

INNOVATION

As you have seen in this chapter, innovation is fundamental to establishing and maintaining your differentiation. There are different ways to innovate, depending on how you decide to differentiate your business.

The vacuum of innovation

Innovation is about finding new ways of doing things that result in positive change.

It is about creating the best solution, not just being trendier.

Effective innovation and differentiation is not about head-to-head competition; it is not about 'me too' copying – it is about transcending the competition, about being the leader.

By always innovating in your business and by leading the way, you set the standards for your industry. Business owners often worry about putting their innovation out into the marketplace for fear of their competitors copying it. But this is, in fact, exactly what you want to happen. As soon as your competitors are playing the 'me too' game and are focused on copying and catching up with you, you have trapped them in your 'vacuum of innovation'. They leave the road ahead open for you to continue to innovate effectively and to lead the way.

By copying you, your competitors are sending the message to the market that you are the best and they want to be like you.

Innovation is a constant and never-ending process, and it's important that you never get complacent. Assume that your competition is working day and night to innovate their business ahead of yours – this sharpens you for anything that is to come.

While some business books will teach innovation strategies, I have found that these often confuse people and can stifle effective thinking and even innovation itself.

Instead I've found that there are four traits that lead to innovation, and one question that drives it.

The question of innovation

Drive all innovation with this question:

How can I make my customer's life easier, simpler and better?

That's it. Keep the focus on the customers and improving their lives, and you will guide your innovation in an effective direction.

Innovation traits

1. Intense drive

You have to be obsessed with improvement and with creating the best outcomes for your customers, your team and for yourself. 'Me too' business is the easy option, but innovative business is the powerful and rewarding option. It's also the challenging option, so you need to be hungry.

2. Curiosity

'How could we do that better?' 'What's a better way to do that?' 'What more can we do?' 'How can we achieve that with fewer steps?' 'What do our customers really want?'

These are all great questions and the sort that effective innovators continually ask themselves. They are interested and engaged in their businesses, and they are always looking for and are open to new and better ways of doing things.

3. Imagination

Great innovation or game-changing ideas come from thinking beyond the norm. Innovative thinkers suspend judgement initially and keep themselves open to possibility.

4. Discipline

Innovative thinkers know that focus is the goal, and that focus is on making their customers' lives easier, simpler and better.

This requires disciplined thinking so that you aren't chasing every cool idea, but prioritising what will make a real difference, and then focusing resources on executing that exceptionally well. Perfection is when there is nothing left to take away, and good always trumps trendy.

Rather than having a formal framework, many businesses that are great at innovation encourage it with conversation. They make it a part of their everyday thinking, conversation and work. They know great ideas can come from anywhere, so innovation is always on their radar.

SUMMARY

The ideal outcome of Effective Differentiation is to change the status quo of an industry or an industry segment, to influence your industry to perceive you as the authority, or to improve your industry in a meaningful way. When you do this well, you create space for your business to flourish while the competition scrambles to catch up.

When you change how business is done, and you are the only one providing that service or product in the new way, then you have mastered differentiation.

Your competition will try to catch up, but by effectively solving the ongoing and evolving challenges of your customers, you will stay ahead.

Differentiation is critical to any business, and it has to be done right. As you can see from this chapter, it doesn't have to be complicated, but it does take focus and dedication to consciously decide what differentiation strategy your business requires to stand out. Differentiation must be based on the needs and challenges, known or unknown, of your customers, and effective ongoing differentiation needs to keep up with their evolving needs.

You need to be both different and relevant. When you achieve this, you become more and more specialised and leave less and less space for your competitors, who are continually chasing you.

Innovation isn't something you do once and then forget about. You must create a 'vacuum of innovation' if you want to be the leader in your market, trapping your competition into playing catch-up, and leaving the path ahead of you open and free.

This is the essence of the Unfair Fight, because over time your competition gets squeezed out of your market and becomes obsolete.

It leaves you competing only with yourself in continuing to improve.

That's the Unfair Fight.

ROUND 6

Results Marketing

Effective marketing is about delivering meaningful results that grow your business. Many business owners take cues from corporates with massive budgets and think that marketing is all about 'getting our name out there'. This is exactly what the corporates want you to do, because it is ineffective for small- and medium-sized businesses and it is a massive waste of money.

You're not Coke or Nike, so don't advertise like them.

To make a positive impact on your business, your marketing needs to be about delivering tangible results in the form of leads that become customers, and then making customers loyal and doing repeat business with them. Getting your name out there, or branding, is a secondary result of good marketing, not the goal.

The Unfair Fight is about focusing your unique resources in ways that the bigger companies don't have available to them. You will then gain the advantage.

MARKETING WITH INTEGRITY

Too often business owners lead with marketing that isn't backed up with a great business. This strategy will only work in the short term because people will eventually find you out.

Effective marketing must begin with having a product or service that is worthy of attention.

A great business is one you can be proud of, one that makes a positive difference.

You can't put icing on dog shit and call it cake. The same goes with business; your marketing is the icing, so make sure that you have a cake underneath that people will be excited about once they get past the icing – don't let them find themselves neck-deep in dog doo-doo.

The rest of the Unfair Fight is about baking a great cake. This chapter is about dressing that cake up with delicious icing so people want to eat it.

WHY TRADITIONAL MARKETING DOESN'T WORK AND WHY YOUR CURRENT MARKETING PROBABLY SUCKS

Most businesses are wasting their marketing budget on ineffective marketing that only makes the advertising companies rich.

There are three main reasons why traditional marketing doesn't work:

1. Congestion

Consumers are being bombarded by marketing everywhere they turn: it's on their phones, on their TVs, on billboards, in everything they read. It's everywhere.

According to Yankelovich Research, 10 years ago the average consumer received 1 000 commercial messages a day. Even then, that's a lot to cut through. But now the average consumer receives over 3 000 commercial messages per day. As a result, businesses are spending over three times as much money on their marketing than they did a decade ago.

2. Immunity

You know that phenomenon when you move into a new house and you notice all sorts of things that need fixing, then a few months later you haven't fixed them and you don't even notice them any more? That's what's happening with advertising; people are becoming immune to the sheer volume that they are exposed to.

Most of what you have been taught about advertising, even by the advertising greats of the past, is now wrong because of this phenomenon.

Not only are people switching off to advertising, but the promise of big benefits is also failing now – despite marketers still pushing this approach. When this old school of thought was developed, prospects were under-marketed, so the big promises and words like MASSIVE, NEW and INSTANT got people's attention and got them excited.

But today, these same words can trigger instant rejection. These words have been so overused that they scream to your prospects: 'I have a complete lack of imagination, so all I can do is shout at you.' So customers respond the same way they would to any idiot shouting at them – they ignore them.

You can test this on yourself. When was the last time you got excited by a MASSIVE claim, a FREE set of steak knives or the latest, INSTANT RICHES scheme?

You didn't, did you? It's because you've heard such claims too often and you are immune to them.

But do go to www.samhazledine.com to get your FREE steak knives and INSTANT washboard abs in less than 30 seconds per day!

3. Lack of measuring

The last thing an advertising agency wants to do is talk measuring and numbers. They will claim the intangible benefits of marketing are brand awareness – 'You just need to get your name out there' – and you can't measure that or even put a price on it.

Bullshit. The only thing you need is to make a profit from every dollar you spend. You don't have millions of dollars to waste on getting your name 'out there'.

Your new marketing mantra is:

If it can't be measured, it can't be improved.

These are the three reasons why traditional marketing doesn't work for you.

When was the last time you saw an advertising agency actually advertising itself? That's right, never. That's because while they are happy to sell you the Kool-Aid, they certainly aren't going to drink it themselves.

SO WHAT'S THE SOLUTION?

In the late 19th century, a former Canadian mounted policeman turned marketer, John E. Kennedy, coined a great phrase that I think sums up effective marketing for the majority of business owners: salesmanship in print.

Marketing is about understanding buyer psychology – getting a customer to put their hand in their pocket to take out their hard-earned money and give it to you. It's not just about being creative, or clever, or getting your customers to laugh at how witty you are.

Think about your marketing as being your 'salesman in the field'.

Would you send a salesman into a prospect's office and get them to sing a catchy jingle?

Would you get your salesman to go into a prospect's office and sit quietly for half an hour to observe the 'white space' that your advertising agency wants to make an advertisement look pretty?

Would you get your salesman to go into a prospect's office and shout at them and make bold and irrational-sounding claims?

Of course not. But this is exactly what most people are doing with their marketing. If you take just one thing from this chapter, make it to stop thinking about your marketing as 'getting your name out there' and to start thinking about it as your 'salesman in the field'.

Do that, and the rest becomes much easier.

IF IT CAN'T BE MEASURED, IT CAN'T BE IMPROVED

Imagine a doctor diagnosing and treating patients using nothing but gut instinct.

While they might get the diagnosis right some of the time, chances are they will get it wrong most of the time. Furthermore, they won't actually know whether they get the diagnosis right or wrong, so they'll never improve.

The diagnosis determines the treatment they prescribe, so their gut-instinct diagnosis could make the patient better, but it might make them much worse, or even kill them.

This is exactly what is happening to most businesses' marketing. You need to know what's going on, so you need measurements in order to make sure that your marketing does what you want it to do and doesn't kill your business.

You wouldn't see a doctor who didn't believe in tests. That would be silly, wouldn't it? So don't do it with your livelihood.

THE NEW MATH OF MARKETING

Most businesses have a website, and any decent website will have a way of capturing the contact details of prospects. The New Math of Marketing therefore starts with the website, but if you don't have a website, this still applies – you just need to start at the second line.

1. Website visitors x web conversion rate = leads

    (At this point you want to split your leads into market segments)

2. Leads × sales conversion rate = customers
3. Customers × average rand sale × average number of transactions = revenue
4. Revenue × margin = profit

It is important to get as granular as you can with your measuring. A lot of marketing advice talks about 'averages', but this fails to give you the information you need to accurately make decisions and run your business. That's like an aeroplane having a single dial showing the average of all the other dials.

But you don't have to get over-granular, as that can confuse you. To start, make sure that you measure leads by market segment. You can then apply averages beyond that with the confidence that you aren't kidding yourself.

Most business owners want more customers, revenue and profit, so this is what they think they need to measure. However, customers, revenue and profit are all outcomes, not inputs, and while you need to measure them, the more important measures are the factors that contribute to them.

Here are some levers you can pull:

Website visitors
You can take action to drive visitors to your website. There are many ways to do this, including search-engine optimisation, paid advertising, blogging, using traditional advertising to drive people online – the list is endless. Over time you can build a picture of what actions drive more or fewer leads.

Web conversion rate
This is a critical number that most businesses fail to focus on: the number of website visitors divided by the number of leads who give you their details. It is critical, because this transaction is at the start

of the process and therefore underpins everything. A high web conversion rate makes everything else better, and a low web conversion rate makes everything else harder.

Sales conversion rate

This is the first number you need to measure for your sales team. It is the proportion of leads that they convert into customers.

Average rand sale

The second sales number, the average rand sale, is how much you get your average customer to spend.

Average number of transactions

The third sales number, the average number of transactions, is a measure of how many times your average customer buys from you. It's a measure of how loyal they are to you.

Margin

This is a measure of business performance and gives you an insight into how well you turn revenue into profit.

Outcomes

These are the results of the levers you can pull:

- Leads – the number of people who have engaged with your business.
- Customers – the number of people who have purchased from you.
- Revenue – the total amount you have sold.
- Profit – the amount you have left over after your expenses.

MedRecruit spends around $1 million per year on marketing. At one stage our sales were fluctuating, so we did a lot of analysis and found the issue was low leads. At the time I didn't understand the New Math of Marketing, so we invested even more in our marketing to drive up leads.

However, this increased spending only had a small impact on leads, so we realised there was an underlying issue. We dug deeper and found that the website conversion rate since launching a new website had halved. It was no wonder our leads were down – people weren't even getting to us.

With a small change to the registration process we doubled our conversion rate and our leads skyrocketed.

When you pay attention to the New Math of Marketing you won't be surprised by things like this, because you will be on top of the important metrics and you can correct on the fly.

FIVE KEY CALCULATIONS

There are five important calculations you need to make on a regular basis to ensure that your marketing is doing what it's supposed to do.

1. Cost per lead (CPL) = campaign cost divided by leads generated

- This is the amount you spend to get a prospect to either visit you or speak to one of your salespeople.
- If you spend R1 000 on a campaign and you get 10 potential customers to visit you, then your CPL is R1 000 ÷ 10 = R100.
- This is an important leading indicator on how your campaign is going, and that's all it is – your end-goal isn't leads, it's profit. Many marketers forget this.

2. Cost per customer (CPC) = campaign cost divided by the number of customers

- This is the amount you spend to get an actual customer. This is an essential number, as customers are what you want. Too many marketers focus on leads, but leads don't pay the bills.

- Using the previous campaign, if just one of those 10 people who visited you purchased your product or service, then your CPC is R1 000 ÷ 1 = R1 000.
- Again, this is an important leading indicator.

3. Lifetime total value (LTV) = average total revenue per customer = average rand sale x average number of transactions

- This is the total amount of revenue you expect to make from every customer. This is a truly important number. Make sure that you're aware of it.
- Using the previous example again, let's say the average customer spent R10 on an average of four times. The LTV is R10 x 4 = R40. At a R1 000 CPC, this is clearly not sustainable. On the other hand, if the average customer spent R5 000 eight times, then the LTV is R5 000 x 8 = R40 000, which is a much better return on the R1 000 spent.

4. Lifetime profit (LP) = total average profit you expect to make from each customer = (LTV x profit margin) – CPC

- This is the most important number. Focusing on revenue is like business pornography: big is good, but it doesn't really matter. What matters is how much money you actually take home. LP is the amount in your pocket at the end of the day and this is the number that will tell you if a campaign is worthwhile or not.
- Back to the previous example, where the LTV was R40 000. This seems like a great return on R1 000. But if the profit margin was just 1 per cent, then the LP would be R400 (R40 000 x 1 per cent) minus R1 000, and the campaign just lost you R600 per customer. If the profit margin was 20 per cent, then the LP would be R7 000, which is a good return on R1 000. In this case, you could spend

the R1 000 as often as you could generate this return, and that's good business.

5. Return on investment (ROI) = (LP ÷ CPC) x 100

- This is a great measure of how effectively you are spending your money. If your ROI is over 100 per cent, you can keep doing what you've been doing as much as you want and you'll be making money. If your ROI is under 100 per cent, you need to make changes, as you're losing money.
- In the previous example, where the LP was R7 000 with a CPC of R1 000, the ROI is (R7 000 ÷ R1 000) x 100 = 700 per cent.

When you know how much money you make from your customers, and you know how much it costs to acquire them, you essentially enter the game of buying customers, which is also known as legally printing money.

It's important that you start using these calculations on all campaigns you run because then, and only then, can you determine what's working and what isn't, what's making you money and what's losing you money.

The great marketer P.T. Barnum famously said: 'Fifty per cent of my advertising is wasted – I just don't know which 50 per cent.' Well, the New Math of Marketing will tell you exactly that.

It's not complicated, but it does require you to give up your addiction to what I call 'hopeium' – which is that tendency some people have to put their heads in the sand and hope everything will turn out all right – and get granular on the numbers.

There's a lot of maths here that you don't need to do yourself. Register at www.samhazledine.com to download the Campaign Analysis Calculator, which will do the work for you.

WHAT BUSINESS ARE YOU REALLY IN?

Before you embark on any marketing activity, you need to get very clear about what real estate you want to occupy in the minds of your customers.

Many business owners confuse the business they are in with the product or service that they sell.

But remember, people buy on emotion and justify with logic.

The business you are in is therefore the business of emotion. You must first clarify what emotion your customers want to feel by buying your product or service. Then you can target your messaging and marketing, and your entire business, to provide that emotion.

Find out what they want, then give it to them – the simple formula for successful marketing.

How do you find out the emotion they want?

From Round 2, you already know that your customers are buying an emotion, so this won't come as too much of a shock to you – to find out what emotion they want, *just ask them.*

Business owners think they need to lock themselves away in their offices to figure out their customers' needs, but that's nearly impossible unless you can read minds.

Talk to your customers and they will tell you what they want, and therefore what you need to deliver.

You don't need to do expensive market research and conduct focus groups, but you can if you want. I'm not saying market research doesn't work, but you can simply ask them questions yourself:

- Why do you use our product?
- What are the benefits of using our product?
- How does that make you feel?
- Why do you *really* use our product?

That's it. Talk to your customers and they will tell you everything you need to know.

Remember, the CEO of your big corporate competition is sitting in her office conducting brainstorming and think-tank sessions to figure out her customers. You have just gone direct to the source.

Innovation happens when you get in front of the people you are trying to benefit, not when you are locked away in your office.

YOUR UNIQUE CLIENT ADVANTAGE

The key to creating your Unique Client Advantage (UCA), from which everything else stems, is to focus your message and eliminate the noise. It is about elegantly expressing the business you are in so people know exactly what benefit they get so that they will take the action you want them to take.

Unique

Your UCA must stand out, otherwise it will get lost in the 'noise' of the other 3 000 messages your prospects are bombarded with each day. For most businesses whose product or service has become a commodity, their uniqueness will often be a demonstration of how well they understand their customers. If your product or service is truly the only one of its kind in the world (unlikely), then this should be expressed.

Client

This is about them, not about you. Full stop.

Advantage

Advantage has to be seen from the point of view of your customers, as something that benefits them. Advantage can't just be unique.

What stage your business is at, and how well your customers know you, will determine where you position your UCA, as either:

- What you do.
- How you do it.
- Why you do it.

The further down you go, the closer you get to 'why', the more your UCA will be aligned with the emotion you are trying to give your customers, and the more 'unique' your UCA will be.

What you do

At this stage it is very difficult to be unique because you probably have competition that essentially provides a very similar product or service as you. If you're not totally unique, you can't use this as a marketing strategy. Some people try to dress up this lack with super-latives, but this is not recommended, as it is seen as disingenuous.

For example, if you run the only Indian restaurant in Pofadder, then your UCA might be 'Pofadder's only Indian restaurant'. If there are three Indian restaurants in town, dressing up your business as 'Pofadder's BEST Indian restaurant' doesn't cut it.

How you do it

Taking it a step deeper … For new companies or companies creating a new industry, this can be a great place to position your UCA so people can immediately understand your business.

You must be careful here that you don't mistake how you do things with industry 'hygiene', which customers just expect. For example, 'service with a smile' is what people expect, so don't claim that as your point of difference.

An example from one of my businesses, Pick-a-Medic, was when we created a new product that essentially flipped medical recruitment on its head and put hospitals in control of finding doctors who met their needs. This saved them large amounts of both time and money. For Pick-a-Medic we developed the UCA 'Doctors at Your Fingertips', which is essentially how we were making the doctors available. We positioned the company this way because we needed to give the hospitals some idea of how the product worked, because it was completely new to them.

Another good example comes from Ford Motor Company. Between 1979 and 1982, they lost $3 billion – American consumers weren't buying American cars because they had perceived, accurately, that Japanese cars were of superior quality. Then Ford's chairman, Philip Caldwell, saw a TV show about the rise of Japanese industry. After World War II, Japan's industry was in disarray and couldn't produce anything of quality. American business strategist W. Edwards Deming was brought in to help them get into shape. He believed that the American business practice of cutting costs until you can't cut any further was hurting businesses there, and he believed that a commitment to quality would always pay off in the long term.

Deming instilled this belief into Japanese business; they adopted the practice of *kaizen*, the philosophy of constant and never-ending improvement. As a result, Japanese business flourished and they became known for their superior-quality goods.

When Caldwell learnt this, he brought Deming to Ford, and they adopted this practice. By 1986 Ford had turned around from losing billions to being America's most profitable car company.

They adopted the UCA: 'Ford: Quality is Job One.'

This UCA was entirely appropriate because it addressed the core message they needed to get across to their American consumers, and it revitalised a struggling company.

Why you do it

This is where I recommend most businesses aim to position their UCA. This is where you can demonstrate that you understand your customers' real needs, their emotional needs. In itself this approach is unique because most businesses don't know what their customers' emotional needs are. This is a true advantage for your customers, because they can be confident that they will get what they really want from your business.

For example, in 2013, we positioned MedRecruit's UCA as 'Love Your Work'. It states the benefit doctors will gain by working with MedRecruit, and it's also a way of showing them our appreciation. Our UCA is unique because it is not only very different from every other recruitment company's, but it also demonstrates that we understand our customers and are committed to creating the best outcomes for them. It also relates to our vision of 'Enrich Lives'.

A STARVING CROWD

If I asked 100 restaurant owners 'What is the one thing you would want that would guarantee your success?' I guarantee I would get 100 different answers.

Some would want the best recipe, others the best ingredients, others the best view, others the fastest service, others the best-looking wait staff, and so on.

And if they could magically have all those advantages and I could only have one, then I guarantee that I could still beat all of them with the one advantage I would choose:

A starving crowd.

Think about it, what will you eat when you are absolutely starving? Anything. If you hadn't eaten for three days and someone put a burger in front of you, would you ask about the ingredients, would you look at the waitress, would you check out the view from the window?

No way. You'd dig in, you'd eat, and you'd be incredibly satisfied.

I have seen countless businesses go broke because they lacked this key ingredient – they didn't have a starving crowd.

If there are 20 restaurants and one customer, and that customer is not even hungry, is that a game you want to be in?

No way.

You must find a niche market that is hungry, that has a need that isn't being met. You need to find your starving crowd. This is so important that if you can't find your starving crowd, then you need to seriously think about whether you want to be in that particular business.

WHAT THE MARKET WANTS ⟷ **THE GAP (YOUR STARVING CROWD)** ⟷ **WHAT THE COMPETITION IS DELIVERING**

Find out what the market wants

You know what you need to do … It's a core strategy that you'll hear over and over in this book: *ask them*. Talk to your customers.

Henry Ford famously said that if he'd asked people what they wanted, they would have said, 'A faster horse.'

The moral is, don't just ask your customers about what they want, get inquisitive and find out *why* they want it. What are they trying to achieve?

If Henry Ford's customers had said they wanted a faster horse, then all he had to do was ask one more question and he'd have had the answer to what they really wanted.

That question is: 'Why?'

If he'd asked 'Why?', they probably would have said, 'To get places faster.' I am sure that he did ask this question, if not to others then at least to himself, because he got to the right answer: the gap is to get to places faster. Ford discovered this and went about building his solution and revolutionising the world.

Asking 'Why' will get you there.

Find out what the market is already getting

It's important to find out what your competition is already providing to your customers. This is really easy to do.

- Online – their websites will tell you a huge amount and online is the place to start.
- Mystery shop – try out their product and service for yourself.
- Ask your customers – some will have used the competition, so ask them about their experience.

This doesn't have to be complicated, but it does have to be done, so get to it.

Figure out the gap

Now that you know what your customer wants and you know what your competition is giving them, you can figure out the gap; the space between what they want and what they are getting.

This is your starving crowd.

In Round 5, you learnt in detail how to cook up a meal that will satisfy your customers and keep them coming back for more.

So feed them.

When I started MedRecruit, I found a starving crowd – doctors wanted to create a great lifestyle in medicine, but no one was helping them to do it. Because I focused on this, our business became the fastest-growing service business in New Zealand in 2009.

But, as every other agency caught on, the crowd started to become satiated. At that point we were in conversation with the hospitals and found that we had a starving crowd there, too. While the hospitals were being sent a lot of CVs, they weren't getting quality doctors and, as a result, they were wasting huge amounts of time trawling through the literature.

We created a business model that gave doctors to the hospitals in the form of solutions, not lots of options. The hospitals loved this, and our business grew. And because the hospitals chose to use MedRecruit doctors first, we were able to satisfy the starving doctor crowd by alleviating their pain of having to sign up with multiple agencies to increase their chances of getting work.

Keep the conversation with your customers going, as the starving crowd can become satiated and, if you don't evolve to find the new hunger, then you will join your competition.

Why is the starving crowd so important?

There's another reason why finding your starving crowd is critical to your success: they are the ones who are listening and who will spread the word about your product or service.

In the past, marketers would aim for the early and late majorities, but that's a dangerous strategy now that being constantly bombarded with messages has made those majorities immune to marketing.

The innovators and the early adopters are the ones who are interested; they are open to new ideas. Market to those people, because they are more likely to pay attention and spread the word.

The majority likes to play it safe, but safe doesn't get noticed. Safe is therefore risky. Be bold and go after the starving crowd, because that's the way to get traction with your marketing.

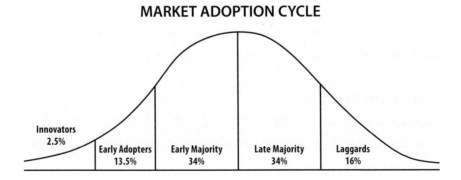

MARKET ADOPTION CYCLE

Innovators 2.5% | Early Adopters 13.5% | Early Majority 34% | Late Majority 34% | Laggards 16%

BRANDING OR DIRECT RESPONSE?

As I've said, advertising agencies will go on about your brand and getting your brand 'out there'. Direct-response marketers spit on the feet of brands, claiming that direct-response marketing principles are all that matter.

But remember that both groups are trying to sell you something.

The truth is that branding without direct response is ineffective, and direct response without branding is naive.

You need both to be really effective.

HOW TO CREATE AN EFFECTIVE BRAND

Everything in this chapter, in fact in this entire book, will help you to create a great brand, because a brand is about being known for something and having a reputation for delivering what customers want.

In addition, there are three things you can do to make it even better:

1. Make it unique

Make sure that your brand helps you to stand out from the crowd, and make sure you do it in a way that also supports your key messages and appeals to your target customers. Remember that being unique must be grounded in meeting your customers' needs, not just being one of a kind or standing out just for the sake of it.

2. Reflect reality

Make sure that your brand reflects your unique culture, your style and your service. Your brand must be based in reality.

3. Message Stacking

Reinforce your brand with everything you do. Make sure that all the touch points – from prospect to client to repeat client – reinforce your message and your brand.

I call this Message Stacking, where everything builds on the previous step to create a stronger impression on your customers.

Your brand is a small but fundamental part of your marketing mix, and by applying these three incredibly simple principles, alongside having a great business, you can create a strong brand that reinforces the direct-response marketing principles you apply.

DIRECT-RESPONSE MARKETING PRINCIPLES THAT WORK CONSISTENTLY

Direct-response marketing is actually quite easy to combine with your brand to create really effective marketing. Combining the two is simply making sure that you use the direct-response principles, contained in the following section, in conjunction with consistently using your brand in a way that customers can get to know and trust.

I have spent countless hours studying direct-response marketing, and I have discovered some very effective principles. But it's like the 80:20 rule: 20 per cent will get you 80 per cent of the results.

What follows are the 20 per cent of principles that deliver most of the results.

Use AIDA

AIDA is one of the oldest and most effective formulas for writing advertisements. It stands for Attention – Interest – Desire – Action.

First you must grab the Attention of your customer. It doesn't matter how good everything else is if you can't get people's attention.

Once you've got their Attention, you need to build and keep their Interest. A great way to do this is to be clear on the benefits to the customers. Another great way is to spell out what they are going to get from continuing to read your advertisement.

Now that they are interested, you need to build their Desire. This is achieved by appealing to them emotionally. Decide what emotion you want to appeal to: love and acceptance, respect, self-esteem, etcetera, and build that emotion with your copy. You can also highlight the customers' frustrations, then build the vision of what life will be like when they buy your product or service and remove those frustrations.

Now it's time to get the reader to take Action. Tell them exactly what to do to fulfil their desires.

Get attention with a great headline

The headline of any advertisement is the part that is most read, so make it great, using these seven steps to writing killer headlines:

1. Appeal to your audience's emotions

Because you now know that all people buy on emotion and justify with logic, it's a great idea to appeal to the emotion that people will feel using your product or service. Make things easier, quicker, simpler, unravel a problem, offer an emotional benefit.

2. Use numbers

Numbers in headlines work because they get people's attention and interest them in finding out more.

3. Use interesting trigger words

Find the adjectives that appeal to your target customer and use them. It's important to match the adjective to your audience. Be careful about overdoing it and activating your potential customers' bullshit meter. Some good examples are effortless, easy, fun, free, essential, absolute, etcetera.

4. Use unique rationale

Consider giving readers reasons, facts, lessons, ideas or secrets. These also elicit interest and make people want to find out more.

5. Start with 'how to'

How-to headlines offer the promise of solid information and solutions to problems. They identify with a reader's pain and offer the possibility of a solution to that pain.

6. Make a big promise

Promise the reader something of real value to them. You are daring your reader to read on, to find something he or she really wants.

7. Test

Try out at least a couple of headlines and measure which one gives you the best response.

A great formula for writing a good headline is:

Number/Trigger Word + Adjective + Keyword + Promise.

For example, if you are selling dog shampoo, in the past you might have used a headline like this: 'Ways to Effectively Clean Your Dog'.

Apply this formula to make it: '7 Easy Ways You Can Bathe Your Dog at Home'.

If you have a dog, which one is more likely to encourage you to read on?

Always provide an irresistible offer

There are six types of offers, and you need to include one or more in all your marketing:

1. A discount: 50 per cent off.
2. More for your money: buy one, get one free.
3. A free trial: 30-day free trial.
4. An extra: pay for the standard product and get an upgrade to the premium product.
5. A diagnosis to then prescribe a solution: a free audit.
6. Free information or educational material: a how-to guide (see 'The Monkey's Fist' on page 153).

You must ensure that your offer is crystal clear and people know exactly what they are getting. It must be both good value and have a logical reason behind it – a believable reason for the offer boosts response.

> *'Make your offer so great that only a lunatic would refuse to buy.'*
> – CLAUDE HOPKINS

Always provide a reason to respond now

Make sure that you build in scarcity to get your prospects to take action now: an expiry date, limited availability or a bonus for a fast response all work well to create urgency and to get the prospect to act.

People want things the most when there is a chance they might not be able to have them. If you have a hard deadline beyond which no orders will be accepted, then mention it. If there are a limited number of items you can sell, tell people. If there are only a limited number of spaces, share it.

And make sure that you are true to your word. Don't fudge it or make exceptions, as that will undermine your integrity and your effectiveness in future marketing.

Always be clear on how to respond

Make sure that there is a strong, clear, easy-to-understand call to action. Tell the prospect exactly what they need to do and when. Do you want them to call you, to visit your website or come in to your shop? Tell them exactly what is expected. And tell them when they need to do it. Leave nothing to chance.

Always follow up

Good direct-response marketing always follows up. Countless studies have shown that generally two mailings get double the response of one mailing, and three mailings get triple the response. Make sure that your advertising is not done on its own but is part of a multi-step campaign, because that will deliver better results.

Avoid selling more than one thing at a time

Unless you are selling a group of closely related items, or you have a catalogue, it is best to sell one item and to sell it thoroughly. You might think that selling multiple items will appeal to more people, but the reality is that too much choice causes people to lose interest and you sell less.

Always provide a premium version

A percentage of people always want the best. So make sure that you have a premium version. In general, the premium version will have higher profit margins so you make more money, and you give more people what they want. You also switch the decision from a yes–no choice to an A or B choice, which has been shown to boost your response and will help you sell more of the lower-priced version, too. The law of contrast also comes to your aid here by making the premium version more expensive and thereby making the lower-priced version appear to be great value.

Use a price ending in '7'

Everyone seems to offer a price that ends in '95'; however, the great marketer Ted Nicholas has tested pricing extensively and reports that prices ending in the number '7' work better than any other number.

Don't forget the 'PS'

The PS is the second-most read part of any advertising, so use it to reinforce the most important part of your message, which is contained in your headline.

THE MONKEY'S FIST – THE IRRESISTIBLE FIRST STEP

In his bestselling book *How I Raised Myself from Failure to Success in Selling*, Frank Bettger shared a story that turned him from a struggling salesman into one of the greatest life-insurance salesmen of all time.

While standing on a dock in Miami, Bettger saw the large ships coming in to dock and wondered how the seamen could get the huge ropes, as thick as a man's thigh, from the ship to the dock.

He saw that the seamen didn't even try to throw the heavy rope, known as a hawser; instead, they would hurl a thin rope with a knot at the end weighted with a small lead ball, called a monkey's fist.

A longshoreman standing on the pier would catch the monkey's fist and would pull it in. The thin rope was attached to the thick hawser, which would then be pulled in.

That's how they got the big, unwieldy hawser from the ship to the dock.

In every sale, either in print advertising, or in person, there are at least two sales to be made.

The main sale of your product or service is what most people focus on, but before you even get the chance to sell your main product, you must first sell your prospects on hearing you out; in other words, giving you a chance to sell to them.

Throwing the hawser to shore is too big a first step for any sailor, just as it's too big a first step for you as a marketer to try to sell your product or service ice-cold to your prospects.

Have you been trying to get your prospects to buy instantly from your advertising? Have you wondered why your marketing hasn't been working?

The great New Zealand marketer Richard Petrie taught me this, and it's one of the most reliable and effective ways I have ever learnt to open and then close sales, both in advertising and in person.

You have to make the first step both irresistible and easy to take.

This means that with whatever form of advertising you are using to sell – online, in print, in person – you don't start off trying to sell your product or service. You should start with something that your prospects find desirable and easy to say 'Yes' to; a small commitment they can't resist that leads logically to the bigger commitment of the sale.

The example Richard shared with me was from the early days of door-to-door coffee salesmen. While this is an example from the past, I'm using it because it's a great example of how this method has been used successfully for decades; it worked then and it still works now.

After experimenting with many different approaches, the coffee marketers found the easiest way to sell coffee was by first throwing a Monkey's Fist.

A salesman would knock on the door and, when the woman of the house opened it, they would say, 'Good afternoon, madam, today I bring you a special gift, a half-pound of our finest coffee. Please accept it with my compliments. In around a week I'll return to see what you think of it. Is that all right?'

Who could refuse such an offer?

The next week the salesman would return with the offer of another gift, which was available if an order was placed.

Making the sale this way was easy, because the salesman by-passed the automatic rejection that comes when people feel they are being sold to. As the marketing great Claude Hopkins put it: 'Any apparent effort to sell creates corresponding resistance.' And as Sir Isaac Newton put it: 'For every action there is an equal and opposite reaction.'

The harder you sell up front, the more people will resist.

In the martial art aikido, you meet resistance by moving with it. The Monkey's Fist meets resistance by making it not only easy for people to catch your offer when you throw it to them, but by making it irresistible when you get your offer right.

There are countless ways you can use a Monkey's Fist in your marketing: a free sample, a free diagnosis, audit or check-up, or the method I have found to be most effective: free information or education.

Offering your prospect a report or information that is extremely useful to them gives them tangible benefits that they can't get anywhere else. The great thing about a report is that it gets your prospect to take the first step with you, and the information also moves them towards the obvious choice of your solution.

When I started MedRecruit, we didn't lead by telling people how great we were; we began by marketing 'The Doctors' Definitive Guide to Locuming'. This was the small sale that would earn us the trust of the doctors so we could then talk to them about the big sale, which was actually placing them in a new job.

But beware: Do not offer free information and then send a sales brochure. The information must be of use to your prospect whether or not they use your product or service. But do make your product or service the most attractive proposition for them.

To get immediate access to my unpublished chapter, 'The Three Core Drivers of Success: How to Guarantee Success', register at www.samhazledine.com.

You will also get access to a video of how I have used these strategies to create success in my own life, repeatedly, and how you can, too; how I became the New Zealand extreme ski champion; how I created New Zealand's

fastest-growing business-services business; and how
I did all that while creating a happy family.

I followed a process that can be applied by
anyone to achieve success in anything.

But only register and watch the video if you are truly committed
to creating success in your life, because if you aren't, it will be
uncomfortable. But if you are committed, it will be inspirational,
as you will learn the formula to create success repeatedly.

If you don't do this, success could be hard to attain;
if you do it, then success is inevitable.

THE EFFECTIVE JOURNEY: KNOW ME, LIKE ME, TRUST ME, BUY ME

You don't just get married to someone the first time you meet them; you engage in a little flirtatious conversation, you share stories, you get to know each other, you date, you get engaged, and then you get married – it's a journey.

Or in my case, you pose as a sock salesman and sell your future mother-in-law a pair of ski socks, then ask her daughter out while the socks are being purchased ... but that's another story.

Much like the Monkey's Fist is a way to get a prospect to take the first step, your marketing must be approached strategically to take your prospect on a journey from cold to sale.

I was with Keith Cunningham in Texas one time and we were talking with a group of business owners about marketing. At one point Keith got up and walked over to a white board, and on it he wrote: 'Know me, like me, trust me, buy me'. Sometimes the best ideas are so simple, and Keith has kindly given me permission to share this idea with you here.

Know me

Before anyone can become a customer, they must know that you exist. Seems obvious, right? But many business owners sit around waiting for customers to come to them.

'Our product does the marketing for us' is a naive and dangerous position to take as a business owner.

So how do you become known?

1. Get clear on your target audience

This is the most important strategy; there's no point fishing for tuna in a lake. So get crystal clear on your ideal target audience and tightly position your content for them, then market where that target is. Develop a persona for your ideal target customer, then tailor your marketing to them. Don't fall into the trap of trying to appeal to everyone. Stay focused.

2. Be an expert in your niche

Deliver information that positions you as an expert in your niche. The person or business that educates the market, owns the market. And if you deliver this sort of content, people are more likely to share it with other people, who are other prospective customers; in fact, it's great to encourage people to share your content.

3. Build relationships with key influencers

It's not who you know but *who knows you* that is important. Build mutually beneficial relationships with the most important people in your niche, then engage them with your business and target market.

4. Use PR
Be outrageous, do the unexpected, pull stunts that get you on page one of the paper. It's a cheap way to get known, and when done well, you can amuse people and get them to begin liking you.

Like me
Once you are known, you need people to like you. If you are thinking who to invite to dinner, are you going to invite the person you dislike or the one you like?

How do you become liked?

1. Be authentic
Express your unique voice through your marketing.

2. Be real and make it personal
Put your face on your business and tell your personal story. People engage with people, not companies, so share your passions, stories and challenges, and give people an insight into the person or people in your business.

3. Be nice
Treat people well, don't bad-mouth competitors, and your target audience will appreciate you.

4. Be relevant
Understand the real needs of your target customers, then communicate in a way that shows you understand them.

5. Initiate a two-way conversation
People like conversations; they don't like lectures, so engage in a conversation with your target customers.

6. Be generous
Share really valuable information that your potential customers can benefit from before they buy from you.

Trust me
Trust is key for people taking the step from the first sale, the small easy commitment, to the second sale of your actual product or service. How do you become trusted?

1. Over-deliver
Give your target customers more than they expect. Be consistently excellent, keep exceeding people's expectations and they will grow to trust you and believe you will deliver on what you say you will.

2. Deliver on promises
If you say you are going to do something or follow up at a certain time, do it. Do not disappoint your target customers.

3. Use social proof
Share stories of real people who have got great results with your product or service. People are much more likely to believe another customer who recommends your product and service than to believe you blowing your own trumpet.

4. Don't hard-sell
Give your target customers space to make the decision whether to buy from you or not. While the hard sell might work once, it will totally undermine any trust your customer has in you and you will lose a longer-term customer.

5. Offer a guarantee

Guarantees say that you stand behind your product and reduce the risk for people to try you out. I talk more about guarantees and how to create them on page 168.

Buy me

Once people know you, like you and trust you, there is still one further step.

Ask for the sale.

While hard selling is not a good long-term strategy for any business, it is important to ask people for the sale because if you don't ask, you generally don't get.

Round 7, New Sales, covers the sales process in depth (see page 189).

WHERE TO ADVERTISE

Where you advertise is going to be very specific to your business and, more importantly, to your target market. There is no one formula that works for everyone.

Remember, if you want to catch the big fish, you need to go where the big fish are swimming. Selecting the right channel can mean the success or failure of your business, so it's important to get it right.

How to determine your specific marketing channels

Think about your customer and your product or service as we look at the different channels available to you and what is most appropriate.

Type of customer

Are you selling to an individual consumer or to a business customer? Do they want to find you on the internet, or do you need a more personal approach? Think about how your customer wants to buy your product or service, then make sure the marketing channel you choose supports this.

Where your customers are

Where are your customers and what are they already looking at? Are they online? What websites do they frequent? Can you get a mailing list? What other products are they commonly buying, and can you look at the marketing channels those businesses use?

Don't make the mistake of trying to change the behaviour of your customers when it comes to your marketing – just go to where they already are.

What you are selling

Your actual product or service will have a large impact on what channels you choose. Is it a product or is it a service? Is it top end or cheap? It is exclusive or open to anyone?

Online

Almost every business will benefit from an online presence. A website is a cost-effective way for you to really target the customers you want, and many businesses can benefit from a social media presence, too.

There are literally thousands of books written on this subject, but my belief is that most business owners are wasting their time creating a website themselves; you're not a web expert, so get someone who is, because it will save you huge amounts of time, money and brain damage.

In this section I'm giving you enough information to engage the experts to do this for you cost-effectively.

What do you want your website to achieve?

Before you start working on your website, it's important to figure out its purpose. Just getting an online presence is what most businesses strive to do, but that's not an effective strategy; it's important to have a specific outcome for what you want to create, your target.

If you engage someone else to build your website, which I think is a good idea, then be very careful. In my experience, most web designers think the purpose of a website is to show off how creative they are. This is most certainly not your website's purpose.

Possible options for the purpose of your website are to:

1. sell your product or service;
2. generate leads; and
3. establish your credentials.

Figure out why you want a website, then build it to deliver. If you do that, you are more likely to have a successful website. If you don't, then you almost certainly will be wasting your time and money.

Developing your website

1. Determine your domain name

Check if the domain name you want is available on a site like www.godaddy.com and buy it. Aim to get your business name or something that describes what your business does.

2. Build your website

Unless you're already an expert at this, get a web developer to build your website.

What specifically does your website need?

1. Give people a certainty of success

When someone lands on your home page, you've got about three seconds to grab their attention. In that time you need to give visitors certainty of success by telling them what you do, telling them why you are unique, demonstrating any benefits to them, and removing their risk, potentially using a guarantee or a promise.

2. Use a Monkey's Fist

Just as with any other form of marketing, you want to make it easy for the customer to say 'Yes' before trying to sell your product or service.

3. Capture their details

Only a very small percentage of people are looking to buy right now, when they visit your website, so make sure that you have a way to capture their names and email addresses so that you can continue to communicate with them in the future. Generally, you will have to trade an offer (like the Monkey's Fist) for their details.

Check out www.medrecruit.com and www.samhazledine.com if you want to see all of these working well together.

4. Add new content regularly

Providing new content shows your customers you are an active and trustworthy business. You can do this with a blog, or by posting videos or articles regularly. Adding content also improves your website's ability to be found on search engines.

5. Gain customer trust

Tell the story of your business in the 'About' page, giving customers an insight into who you are and what you stand for. Provide customer testimonials and display your phone number on every page if you want them to call you.

6. Generate site traffic

Your priority is to get your site to appear first in Google's organic search results. You can do this by using strategically chosen key words, regularly updating your content, providing internal links and being linked to from other websites. It takes time to achieve this, so, in conjunction, use paid advertising on Google, which can generate traffic instantly.

In my experience, many small business owners try to create an online presence themselves to save money. This is a poor use of resources – get an expert involved, as the time you spend on this is time you can better spend on other areas of your business. Now that you are educated about what you need, you will be able to engage the right expert and direct them effectively.

Social media

Social media can be a great way to promote your business through real-time conversations that are happening every day and are defining your market and brand, whether you choose to participate or not. Those real-time conversations can be harnessed, monitored and measured so that you can actively drive relevant conversations about your business.

Many people think social-media marketing is about creating a Facebook page and randomly tweeting on Twitter; it's not. You want to create a return on your investment, so it's important to decide on which engagement strategy is needed to ultimately drive sales.

There are two main strategies that generate the most returns when it comes to your social-media campaign: marketing engagement and servicing engagement.

Marketing engagement is all about driving brand management and brand awareness while connecting with customers. It's about doing fun things online that engage with your customers, which allows them to feel connected to you. Does this drive sales? Probably, but it can be hard to measure, so I'm not a massive fan.

Servicing engagement is about troubleshooting problems, about providing customers with a way to access help in a place where they are spending a lot of their time. An added benefit is showing that you are transparent and proactive in providing support to your customers.

Social-media marketing is all the hype, but I have seen very few businesses that actually generate much money from it. If you don't want to get left behind, then by all means go on Facebook and Twitter, but be careful about spending too much time there, as it can be seductive and returns on investment can be hard to come by.

Direct mail

Direct mail is a highly targeted way to reach your ideal customers. If you can get a mailing list of your specific customers, and your target market is very specific, then this can be a very effective method of advertising.

It can be very expensive, so use all the core principles of effective direct-response marketing to make this approach pay off (see page 148).

Classified advertising

Classified advertising is a very cost-effective way to use direct marketing without the large expense of direct mail. The great thing about the people who read the classifieds is that they are often looking to buy, so you have a captive, and potentially starving, crowd.

You can run classified advertisements online and also in the more traditional channels like newspapers, magazines and trade journals.

With classified advertisements it's important to measure your results and to try out different ads to see what gives you the best response.

Radio

Radio can be a good medium when your target market is very broad in a specific geography– for example, a hardware store selling a range of products.

Many business owners make the mistake of using radio for branding. Think about radio in the exact same way as any other form of marketing and apply the core direct-response principles.

Television

Television is a very expensive form of high-prestige advertising, which is what sucks many business owners in. If you have a product that appeals to a wide target audience, then this *might* be something for you to consider.

If you use this form of media, then target specific shows that have audience psychographic profiles that match your target customers. Never let the network choose when to run your ads, because that's like rolling the dice.

EXPAND WHAT YOU SELL

You have learnt about the lifetime total value (LTV) of customers because, along with lifetime profit (LP), this is what you should be focusing on as a business owner (see page 137).

Most marketers spend all their time chasing new leads, and in fact they can get obsessed. But the reality is that repeat business from current clients is many times easier to get than new business from new clients.

I fell into this trap, until I found that we already had almost half the doctors in Australasia in our database. Once we realised this, we focused a lot more on communicating with them to help make positive changes in their careers.

There's no question that for high growth (in excess of 50 per cent yearly growth) you need new leads, but to get incremental growth, and even to support massive growth, another strategy you can adopt is to broaden what you sell.

So how can you expand what you sell?

Repeat sales

Focus on building long-term relationships so that your customers will return for repeat business. Apply the four rules for creating a Remarkable Client Experience to achieve this:

1. Never treat a potential customer better than you treat a current customer.
2. The customer, not you, determines what is remarkable.
3. What is remarkable for one customer is not remarkable for another.
4. Surprise.

Related sales

Look for other products or services you could sell your customers. If you're selling books, can you also offer audio programmes and seminars?

Check out the additional resources that you can access to accelerate your business growth at www.samhazledine.com.

Parts and servicing

Almost any product you sell will require some form of servicing over time. Right now, if you just provide the product, consider providing its servicing, too. If you can, set the servicing up at the time of the sale so that it happens automatically. For example, if you sell automatic garage doors, you could set the customer up for yearly inspections and maintenance. This is a great way to generate ongoing and predictable income.

YOUR GUARANTEE

The purpose of a guarantee is to reduce the perceived risk to the consumer from buying your product or service.

Many business owners are worried about providing a strong guarantee for fear of what it might cost them. But in my experience, only about 1 to 2 per cent of your customers will take you up on a guarantee. If you build a good business, that number can be much lower. At MedRecruit, only 0.06 per cent of people took us up on our guarantee.

A strong guarantee works if you have a good product or service, because a potential customer who has never done business with you may be hesitant to purchase if they don't have a way to backtrack if they feel unsatisfied. A good Monkey's Fist will reduce hesitancy because you are educating them, which means they will see you as an expert, and a strong guarantee can give them the added confidence to try you.

Six steps to creating a powerful guarantee

1. Offer a more attractive guarantee than any of your competitors
If you can offer a stronger guarantee than your competitors then your customers are likely to perceive your business as better, or as lower-risk.

2. Make your guarantee very clear and specific
Don't be vague: make sure the customers know exactly what's being offered and exactly how their risk is reduced.

3. Avoid conditions

The more conditions you have, the more you dissipate the effectiveness of the guarantee. Remember that only 1 to 2 per cent of customers will take you up on the guarantee, so be bold and don't water it down with 'fine print'.

4. Raise their eyebrows

Far exceed the customers' expectations so that even if the initial sale doesn't work out, they end up better off. Money back plus more.

5. Ask your customers what's important to them

Ask your customers what's important about your product or service and they will tell you what you need to guarantee. Then guarantee the results that your customers want, not meaningless things.

6. Test your guarantees

Try out a few guarantees with your customers and see what works best.

At MedRecruit, we offered what was perceived as a high-risk guarantee; we guaranteed a subjective superior experience or we would give the doctor an iPad. In the two years we ran this guarantee, dealing with thousands of doctors, we only gave away three iPads; that is, to 0.06 per cent of the doctors we placed.

Remember, the aim of your guarantee is to remove, or at least dramatically reduce, the perceived risk to your prospective customers. You need a great product or service to back up a strong guarantee, so you need to build a good business for this strategy to work. But given that you are reading this book, I assume that you are committed to building a great business. For you, a guarantee is a great tool to increase the response to your marketing.

I guarantee it, or you can have your money back!

WHAT DO YOU HAVE THAT THE BIG CORPORATES DON'T?

This book dissects how you can turn the apparent disadvantage of being a smaller business into a major advantage. Every strategy contained herein can propel your business to the next level because you are more nimble, you can action new strategies quicker, you care more than any corporate and you have a number of tools that just aren't available to the big companies.

Your marketing is no exception. 'Common knowledge' is a very dangerous thing in business and it clouds the ability of big corporates to think clearly and effectively, because they don't want to do anything too different. This chapter gives you multiple ways to do things differently, to think differently and to make your marketing much more effective.

In addition, there are some specific tools available to you that corporates can't emulate.

ADVANTAGE 1 – YOU

That's right, you.

You are a person with a personality. You are unique.

Customers are people and people like to deal with people. You can use yourself in your marketing in ways that corporates just don't do and, in most cases, can't do.

Most small- to medium-sized businesses look at the cold, impersonal corporate advertising and seek to emulate it – big mistake. By injecting your unique personality into your marketing, and your entire business, you give consumers the choice between dealing with a company and dealing with a person. They are much more likely to pick the person if you do it well.

Four key ways to effective 'personal' marketing
1. Be bold and get visible

First, you need to get comfortable with marketing yourself. Don't be afraid. Sometimes this involves putting aside modesty or shyness and stepping into the limelight.

Write your company's blog, communicate with your customers, get front of house. Use your image in your marketing and get videos of you on your website.

This is not a time to shy away from the spotlight.

Being the same as everyone else is unlikely to get you any exposure. Be outrageous, surprise people, do the unexpected and get yourself noticed.

Sometimes it involves donning a leopard-print G-string and water-skiing across a lake in the dead of winter, or visiting the supermarket dressed as Borat, or getting a colonic irrigation … Just look up 'Dare Dr Sam' on YouTube.

In the early days of MedRecruit, we were appealing to junior doctors, who were aged between 25 and 30. We created a competition called 'Dare Dr Sam', where the doctors would dare me to do activities. They would then vote on each activity and I would have to do the one with the most votes. I ended up water-skiing across Lake Wakatipu in a leopard-print G-string in the middle of winter, going to the supermarket in a Borat outfit, careering around town on a bike in a chicken outfit, and experiencing the delights of a colonic irrigation. It all went on YouTube (except the colonic, for obvious reasons) and I got noticed. Media coverage followed, usually accompanied by a large colour photograph.

Most people think that this sort of thing will make others think less of them, but the reality is that most people aren't thinking about you *at all* at the moment, so do something that gets you noticed.

Remember why you're doing it: to grow your business. Successful people do what unsuccessful people aren't prepared to do, so get over your fears and jump in.

2. Get clear on exactly who you are

This might seem strange – you do know who you are, right?

Possibly not in this instance. While you need to act with integrity and not portray yourself as something you really aren't, you also need to be clear on the exact parts of yourself you want to show to your customers, the parts that are going to help them to discriminate in your favour. This is your persona.

A great way to do this is to create a brand archetype so that you deliver a consistent message throughout all your marketing. Gather the back story to the persona and communicate it in a way that your persona would.

An archetype is a character that people can relate to, which symbolises a quality. Most people already understand archetypes, so you can provide your customers with a short cut to getting to know you. The idea behind using a brand archetype is to anchor your brand against something iconic that is already embedded within the conscious and subconscious minds of your audience.

I found a great resource that clearly outlines brand archetypes at www.marketingideas101.com, and the following information has been adapted from this website with their permission.

THE 12 BRAND ARCHETYPES

BRAND ARCHETYPE 1: THE SAGE

'THE SAGE WEARS CLOTHES OF COARSE CLOTH
BUT CARRIES JEWELS IN HIS BOSOM; HE KNOWS
HIMSELF BUT DOES NOT DISPLAY HIMSELF;
HE LOVES HIMSELF BUT DOES NOT HOLD
HIMSELF IN HIGH ESTEEM.'

LAO TZU

The Sage is the wise old master whom people turn to and trust, and whose goal is to use intelligence and analysis to understand the world. The Sage's motto is 'The truth will set you free' and his driving desire is to find the truth. He seeks out information and knowledge through self-reflection, and he fears ignorance.

The chink in the Sage's armour is that he can study the details forever and never act.

The Sage is also known as expert, scholar, detective, advisor, thinker, philosopher, academic, researcher, planner, professional, mentor, teacher, contemplative, guru.

The Sage in the market:
- provides expertise or information to customers;
- encourages customers to think;
- is supported by research-based facts; and
- differentiates from others whose quality or performance is suspect.

ARCHETYPE EXAMPLES: BBC, CNN, Warren Buffett

BRAND ARCHETYPE 2: THE INNOCENT

'INNOCENCE IS ALWAYS UNSUSPICIOUS.'

JOSEPH JOUBERT

The Innocent is full of faith and optimism and her goal is to be happy. Her motto is 'We are young and free so let's love each other' and her driving desire is to achieve utopia. She does the right thing and fears being punished for being bad or wrong.

The chink in her armour is that she can be naive.

The Innocent is also known as utopian, traditionalist, naive, mystic, romantic, dreamer.

The Innocent in the market:

- offers a simple solution to a problem;
- associates with goodness, morality, simplicity, nostalgia or childhood;
- sets fair pricing;
- has straightforward idealistic values; and
- differentiates from brands with poor reputations.

ARCHETYPE EXAMPLES: Dove soap, The Body Shop, Earthchild

BRAND ARCHETYPE 3: THE EXPLORER

'EXPLORATION IS REALLY THE
ESSENCE OF THE HUMAN SPIRIT.'

FRANK BORMAN

The Explorer is ambitious and values autonomy and being true to one's soul. His goal is to experience a better, more authentic, fulfilling life. The Explorer's motto is 'Nothing fences me in' and his driving desire is to be free to find out who he is through exploring the world. The Explorer is on a journey and seeks out and experiences new and exciting things, and he fears being restricted, conformity and being trapped.

The chink in the Explorer's armour is aimless wandering and being labelled a misfit.

He is also known as seeker, wanderer, individualist, pilgrim.
The Explorer in the market:
- helps people to feel free and to be non-conformist;
- is rugged and sturdy and useful in the great outdoors or in dangerous environments;
- helps people express their individuality;
- fosters a culture that creates new and exciting products or experiences; and
- differentiates from a successful regular brand or conformist brand.

ARCHETYPE EXAMPLES: Cape Union Mart, Indiana Jones, Jeep

BRAND ARCHETYPE 4: THE RULER

'HE WHO IS TO BE A GOOD RULER
MUST HAVE FIRST BEEN RULED.'

ARISTOTLE

The Ruler is a responsible leader whose goal is to create a prosperous, successful family or community. Her motto is 'Power is everything' and her driving desire is control. The Ruler exercises her power and fears chaos or being overthrown.

The chink in the Ruler's armour is being out of touch with reality.

She is also known as boss, leader, aristocrat, king, queen, role model.

The Ruler in the market:

- is a high-status product or service used by powerful people;
- empowers people;
- is a market leader offering a sense of security and stability in a chaotic world; and
- differentiates from populist brands.

ARCHETYPE EXAMPLES: Allan Gray, Apple

BRAND ARCHETYPE 5: THE CREATOR

'LIFE ISN'T ABOUT FINDING YOURSELF.
LIFE IS ABOUT CREATING YOURSELF.'

GEORGE BERNARD SHAW

The Creator is imaginative and creative, and his goal is to realise a vision. His motto is 'If you can imagine it, it can be done' and his driving desire is to create enduring value. The Creator develops his artistic skills and fears mediocre vision.

The chink in the Creator's armour is being a perfectionist.

He is also known as artist, inventor, innovator, muse.

The Creator in the market:

- promotes self-expression;
- fosters innovation or is artistic in design;
- works in creative fields like marketing, public relations, the arts, or technological innovation; and
- differentiates from 'do-it-all' brands that leave little room for the imagination.

ARCHETYPE EXAMPLES: Lego, Sony

BRAND ARCHETYPE 6: THE CAREGIVER

'WHEN YOU'RE A CAREGIVER, YOU NEED TO REALISE THAT YOU'VE GOT TO TAKE CARE OF YOURSELF, BECAUSE NOT ONLY ARE YOU GOING TO HAVE TO RISE TO THE OCCASION TO HELP SOMEONE ELSE, BUT YOU HAVE TO MODEL FOR THE NEXT GENERATION.'

NAOMI JUDD

The Caregiver is compassionate and generous, and her goal is to help others. Her motto is 'Love thy neighbour' and her driving desire is to protect and care for others. The Caregiver does things for others, and she fears selfishness.

The chink in the Caregiver's armour is being exploited or being a martyr.

She is also known as saint, altruist, helper, father, mother.

The Caregiver in the market:

- gives customers an advantage;
- supports families;
- nurtures people;
- helps people stay connected with each other and cares about others;
- helps people care for themselves;
- could be non-profits and charities; and
- differentiates with kindness.

ARCHETYPE EXAMPLES: Mother Teresa, Johnson's Baby Shampoo, Salvation Army

BRAND ARCHETYPE 7: THE MAGICIAN

'DREAM NO SMALL DREAM;
IT LACKS MAGIC. DREAM LARGE.
THEN MAKE THE DREAM REAL.'

DONALD WILLS DOUGLAS

The Magician makes the complex appear simple and finds win-win solutions wherever she turns. Her motto is 'I make magic happen' and her driving desire is to understand the laws of the universe, and to understand the truth. The Magician lives by the vision she develops and fears unintended negative consequences.

The chink in the Magician's armour is becoming manipulative.

She is also known as visionary, inventor, charismatic leader, shaman, healer.

The Magician in the market:

- promises transformation;
- embodies new-age quality;
- is consciousness-expanding;
- fosters spiritual connotations;
- uses medium to high pricing; and
- differentiates through expanding people's minds.

ARCHETYPE EXAMPLES: Disney, Pixar

BRAND ARCHETYPE 8: THE HERO

'A HERO HAS FACED IT ALL;
HE NEED NOT BE UNDEFEATED,
BUT HE MUST BE UNDAUNTED.'

ANDREW BERNSTEIN

The Hero is courageous and competent, and his goal is mastery to improve the world. The Hero's motto is 'Where there's a will, there's a way' and his driving desire is to prove his worth through courageous and heroic acts. He is as strong and competent as possible and fears weakness.

The chink in the Hero's armour is being arrogant.

He is also known as warrior, crusader, superhero, soldier.

The Hero in the market:

- invents products that will have a major impact on the world;
- helps people be all that they can be;
- solves major problems;
- has a clear opponent he wants to beat;
- is the underdog or challenger;
- has customers who see themselves as good, moral citizens; and
- differentiates from competitors who have problems following through or keeping their promises ('brand-enemy' positioning).

ARCHETYPE EXAMPLES: Superman, Nike, *Winning the Unfair Fight*

BRAND ARCHETYPE 9: THE OUTLAW

'LOVE IS THE ULTIMATE OUTLAW. IT JUST WON'T ADHERE TO ANY RULES. THE MOST ANY OF US CAN DO IS SIGN ON AS ITS ACCOMPLICE.'

TOM ROBBINS

The Outlaw is radical and outrageous, and her goal is to overturn what's not working. The Outlaw's motto is 'Rules are made to be broken' and her driving desire is revolution. She disrupts, destroys or shocks, and she fears being powerless.

The chink in the Outlaw's armour is walking a fine line and crossing over to the dark side.

She is also known as rebel, revolutionary, misfit.

The Outlaw in the market:

- appeals to people who feel disenfranchised;
- retains values that are threatened by emerging ones;
- creates the path for revolutionary new attitudes;
- often uses low to moderate pricing, but can be high-priced;
- breaks with conventions; and
- differentiates by being significantly different and running their own race.

ARCHETYPE EXAMPLES: Harley-Davidson, Nando's

BRAND ARCHETYPE 10: THE LOVER

'A TRUE LOVER ALWAYS FEELS IN
DEBT TO THE ONE HE LOVES.'

RALPH W. SOCKMAN

The Lover is passionate and committed, and his goal is to be in a relationship with people and to be surrounded by love. The Lover's motto is 'You are the only one, there is no other' and his driving desire is intimacy. He becomes more and more attractive and fears being alone or being unloved.

The chink in the Lover's armour is being so driven to please that he loses his own identity.

He is also known as partner, friend, enthusiast, lover, team-builder.

The Lover in the market:
- helps people belong;
- helps people have fun;
- uses moderate to high pricing;
- fosters a fun-loving organisational structure; and
- differentiates from overconfident brands.

ARCHETYPE EXAMPLES: Victoria's Secret, Tiffany & Co.

BRAND ARCHETYPE 11: THE JESTER

'CHEERFULNESS IS THE BEST PROMOTER
OF HEALTH AND IS AS FRIENDLY TO
THE MIND AS TO THE BODY.'

JOSEPH ADDISON

The Jester is joyful, and her goal is to have fun and to brighten up the world. The Jester's motto is 'You only live once' and her driving desire is to live in the moment and to enjoy every moment to the full. She plays and makes jokes and fears boredom.

The chink in the Jester's armour is being frivolous and wasting time.

She is also known as trickster, joker, comedienne.

The Jester in the market:

- gives people a sense of belonging;
- helps people have fun;
- uses low to moderate pricing;
- is fun-loving; and
- differentiates from self-important, established brands.

ARCHETYPE EXAMPLES: Muppets, Leon Schuster

BRAND ARCHETYPE 12: THE REGULAR GUY/GIRL

'I UNDERSTAND THE COMMON
MAN BECAUSE I UNDERSTAND ME
IN THAT REGARD, AT LEAST.'

VINCE MCMAHON

The Regular Guy/Girl is realistic, empathetic and lacks pretence, and their goal is to belong. Their motto is 'We are all created equal' and their driving desire is to be connected with others. They develop solid virtues, are down to earth and have the common touch, and they fear being left out.

The chink in their armour is losing their identity in an effort to blend in.

They are also known as the person next door, everyman, realist, working man, solid citizen, the silent majority.

The Regular Guy/Girl in the market:
- provides a sense of belonging;
- represents everyday functionality;
- uses low to moderate pricing;
- embodies traditional values; and
- differentiates from elitist or higher-priced brands.

ARCHETYPE EXAMPLES: The Spur, Mr Price, Bruce Springsteen

These archetypes are ideas to get you thinking about your archetype; they are not the only ones that exist. The important thing about archetypes is that they are familiar to people, so your brand gets all the associations that go along with a symbol that people already understand. They also make it easier for you to be consistent with your marketing message, because you are clear about what you stand for.

3. Make people smile

Ultimately everyone wants to be happy, so make sure that you share ideas that make people smile. Once potential customers like you, it's a much easier step to buy from you, and it's also a much harder step to stop buying from you.

4. Challenge the status quo

Don't just say the same things everyone else is saying. If you've got an opinion, share it; while not everyone will agree with you, they will be much more interested in you and a debate is a great way to engage people.

You may not have thought about it until now, but as a small- to medium-sized business owner you are a huge asset to your business when it comes to marketing in a way that develops a personal connection with your target customers. Stop hiding and get visible – your business needs you.

ADVANTAGE 2 – LOCAL CONNECTION

As a small- to medium-sized business, you have a massive advantage with your ability to connect with the local community and to engage with them in ways large corporates struggle to do.

Use this to build loyalty by engaging with local people on a personal level.

This is one area where sponsorship can have a payback through the law of reciprocity. Sponsor events and organisations that you not only believe in, but that will have a lot of your target market in attendance. If you sell school shoes, then supporting your local schools is a great idea. Parents may then choose to buy their children's school shoes at your shop.

Don't be afraid to be a visible part of your local community.

ADVANTAGE 3 – FLEXIBILITY AND ADAPTABILITY

It is unlikely that you have multiple committees through which you have to pass every idea before they get released to market – if you do, get rid of them.

Corporates have multiple departments and multiple levels of management that need to tick things off before they are released. This dramatically increases the time between an idea being born and it reaching the consumer.

This gives you an unfair advantage.

You can make your marketing topical to the events of the day. For example, if there's a natural weather disaster, your next newspaper advertisement could promote a sale to support the people affected. Not only will you engage prospective customers and give them a reason to shop with you, you will also reinforce your position as a local business that understands and cares about local people.

SUMMARY

Marketing done well is effective, conveys your message and puts your business in front of the right people at the right time – it is critical to your success. When you combine great marketing with a great product or service, you will not only grow your business exponentially, but you will create predictable success that will make business a lot more enjoyable.

Stop shooting in the dark and start measuring what's important.

You should aim to measure everything about your marketing so that you know what works and what does not, and you can then continue to improve it.

Position your business in a way that appeals to what customers really want and find your starving crowd, because that's where massive untapped wealth lies.

Stop ineffective branding and start effective direct-response marketing. Support this with an integrated brand that stacks message upon message to move people through getting to know you, getting to like you, getting to trust you, and then to ultimately buying from you.

You have an advantage over every corporate business out there. While you lack the marketing budget, the marketing teams and the global presence they have, you have strategies available to you that can not only neutralise these points, but can give you an unassailable advantage in the niche you are operating within.

As a result, your business and profits will grow exponentially.

And that's the Unfair Fight.

ROUND 7

New Sales

In today's increasingly well-educated and justifiably cynical marketplace, mastering selling requires both a change in mindset and a change in actions.

As markets tighten and businesses get squeezed, the common reaction is to sell harder, to maintain margins and to entrench positions to protect self-serving interests.

The great thing is that as more and more businesses do this, the greater the opportunity for you to move beyond selling as a supplier to providing solutions as a partner.

The more effective you are at this approach, the harder your competition will try and the more they will entrench, further differentiating your business.

The harder they try, the better you do.

That's the Unfair Fight.

Isn't that cool?

THE FUNDAMENTALS OF NEW SALES

First, it's important to understand that selling is no longer the role of one department in a business; it's a team effort.

The marketing department starts the process, the sales department then drives it forward, and finally the delivery department makes it happen.

In small businesses, one person might do all this, but it's still important to think about the steps separately.

Without all departments working together really effectively, it's difficult to move beyond the old way of selling to the new way required in today's market.

Selling is a function of all businesses, so it's critical that you don't leave it to chance. Many business owners have shied away from selling because they see it as manipulative, and the reality is that many sales systems are. But New Sales is a system that elegantly moves your prospect from initial enquiry to becoming a life-long customer who is loyal to your business. New Sales is done with total integrity, and your customer enjoys the process.

New Sales creates two winners: your customer and you.

You can feel really good about New Sales.

SOLUTIONS, NOT SALES

You need to adopt the mindset that your business is not about making sales; it's about providing solutions that are dearly needed by your customers. You are not getting customers to make sales; you are making sales to get customers.

In a highly commoditised market, relationships are key. So the entire New Sales process is about building and deepening relationships.

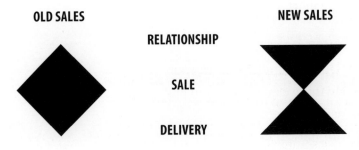

OLD SALES   RELATIONSHIP   **NEW SALES**

SALE

DELIVERY

In the old way of selling, the Sale was the important part, the area that got the most attention and energy.

In New Sales, time and energy are invested in building the Relationship and on Delivery, and the actual Sale is just a point in time that is moved through with very little fuss.

The outcome of this process is that customers don't feel manipulated and sold to; rather, they get excited about the solutions you are providing them and the experience they are getting.

At the core of New Sales is the idea that you never sacrifice a long-term relationship for a short-term gain.

New Sales takes a long-term view of business success, because it understands that short-term success is an illusion.

NEW SALES

Selling is a system, and any system must be adapted to what you are selling.

Unlike many sales systems, New Sales doesn't make the distinction between whether you are selling a product or a service, but it does make the distinction between big-ticket and small-ticket sales.

The reason for this boils down to the time you have available to invest in any individual sale opportunity.

You can look at both systems and determine which one is most appropriate for your business; you have to decide what 'big ticket' and 'small ticket' means to you, and how much time you are prepared to invest to make a sale.

BIG-TICKET SALES
Step 1: Understand the customer

Before anything can happen, you need to intimately understand your customer.

As with most things in *Winning the Unfair Fight*, New Sales starts with the customer and their needs. It is vital that you understand those needs so that you can create solutions that will make your customers excited and addicted to your product or service.

For a long time at MedRecruit, we thought that the customer – the hospital – needed options, in the form of multiple doctors, to fill their vacancies. All agencies operated under this belief, and the rest still do, which led to a massive problem for hospitals. Agencies would race to send through any CV as soon as vacancies were released to the market. As you can imagine, this meant hospitals were inundated with unqualified, poorly matched candidates and would waste massive amounts of time wading through them to find the diamond in the rough.

Our industry's mistaken belief was creating a massive problem for the customer.

When we put ourselves in the shoes of the customer and realised that they needed solutions, not options, and that they were under huge pressure to do more with less, we were able to develop the business to deliver on their true needs.

One solution we created was an online portal, Pick-a-Medic, where hospitals could source candidates and be in total control of the process. They could do this without releasing their vacancies to the market, thereby bypassing the 'agency race' problem. By asking our customers about their needs and then creatively coming up with solutions we were able to design a product that 91 per cent of hospitals said they would use as their first point of call to source candidates for jobs.

By focusing on the needs of the customers, MedRecruit has grown quickly and moved from being a smallish player in a crowded market to being the market leader.

Understanding your customer is *that* powerful. Don't even think about selling until you develop this understanding, and the only effective way to do this is by asking the customer what they need most.

Remember, invention happens in the office and innovation happens in the field. Talk to your customers and let them tell you what they need, then deliver to them in creative ways that differentiate your business and make you the only choice.

Step 2: Lead generation

Once you understand the needs of your customer, it's time to generate leads; this can be done through referrals, marketing or direct selling by approaching prospects in person.

Referrals

Referrals are one of the best ways to generate leads because your customers have done much of the selling on your behalf by the time a new lead makes contact with you. A customer who is thrilled with their experience is the best billboard you can possibly have.

Many businesses leave referrals to chance, trusting that by doing a good job people will naturally refer their friends. This is a fallacy, because while you might spend every moment thinking about your business, chances are that your business is only a small part of your customers' lives. It's your job to encourage the referral process as best you can.

There are two great ways to actively drive referrals:

1. Ask: The first way to drive referrals is to ask your customers for them. While this might seem obvious, my experience is that most businesses don't do it. Ask yourself, when was the last time you asked a customer to refer someone they think could benefit from your service?

When asking, it's important to frame the request in a way that shows you are genuinely looking to help, because that is the only way a current customer is going to refer people they care about to you. You must give your customer certainty that their friends will be grateful about the referral. For example, rather than saying, 'Do you have any friends you can refer to us?', you might say, 'Do you know any people who could benefit from our business in the same way that you have? If you do, it would be great if you could let them know about us. Send them directly to me and I'll look after them personally.'

2. Reward: It's important that you reward people who refer customers to you; it's like anything, if someone does something for you, then you do something for them.

Rewards can take the shape of a formal programme, where people know what they'll get if they refer someone who becomes a customer. In this instance it's important that you give them something that motivates them to refer people – it's got to be something of value. The good thing about this approach is that it can be used to actively drive referral behaviour.

Another way to reward people is by giving them something un-expected to thank them. This can be very powerful because it comes as a surprise and is seen as genuine thanks, rather than a bribe.

Personally I like to use both methods to drive referral behaviour and to say thanks to great referrers.

And always remember to say thank you. A personal hand-written card can be all the reward someone needs.

Marketing

Round 6 is devoted entirely to marketing, and this is how it fits into the sales process.

Marketing is a great way to not only generate leads, but when done effectively, it will pre-select the right people and warm them up so that by the time they make contact with your business, they are fizz-ing and excited about engaging with you.

A very effective way to do this is through the Monkey's Fist education-based marketing method, described in Round 6 (see page 153).

Direct selling

Prospects can be targeted and approached directly. This is a powerful way of reaching your dream customers.

It's important that when you approach people directly, you employ similar principles as you would in effective direct marketing, because really this is just very targeted direct marketing.

The key is to get their attention quickly and make them want to know more.

Step 3: Qualification

If you're selling Lamborghinis, then there's a limited number of people who are potential customers and a lot of tyre-kickers with stars in their eyes.

Before you invest too much time in New Sales, it's important to qualify your prospect as to whether they have:

1. an interest in your product or service; and
2. the ability to purchase your product or service.

Desperate salespeople waste a lot of time with unqualified prospects, hoping to turn everyone who even looks their way into a customer. They are wasting energy on people who are never going to buy, which takes them away from the people who actually might buy, and who are able to buy.

Good salespeople know when their product isn't for that particular customer.

Prepare two or three questions that you can use to quickly rule people out. Think carefully about these questions so that you know definitively whether to rule someone out or not. It's important to remember that effective qualification is about ruling people out, not ruling them in. If someone is not ruled out, then the New Sales system will take them on a journey that will dramatically increase their chances of becoming a customer.

An example from MedRecruit is that when we are talking to international doctors, we have two questions that determine whether they can get medical registration:

1. Where is your medical degree from?
2. How long have you worked in X country?

We can tell from these two questions whether a doctor can get medical registration. If they can't, then we politely inform them that we aren't able to help them at this stage. And, importantly, we let them know what needs to happen before we can help them, and we invite them to get in touch when they meet those criteria. That enables my team to avoid a half-hour conversation that won't go anywhere, thereby saving both our time and the prospect's.

And remember, don't judge too early and don't judge just on appearance. Have the discipline to go through your qualification process because you never know who might become a customer for life.

Just because someone's dressed in shorts and a T-shirt doesn't mean they aren't in the market for a Lamborghini.

Step 4: Develop

Once you have qualified a prospect, it's time to take them on a journey. Develop is the step where you take people who are not only in 'buy now' mode, which is the minority, but people who haven't yet realised they need your product or service, and turn them into customers.

1. Educate first

Today's consumers tend to trust, and therefore buy from, organisations they see as experts. You gain expert status by freely sharing useful information that only you can provide. People love to learn, but hate to be sold to.

Make sure your New Sales system educates your prospects, thereby engaging them and making them want to move forward.

People are open when they are learning, but the moment they feel like you're selling to them, they close up, so don't skip the next few steps. If you do, you are likely to lose the buyer.

2. Focus on the problems you are best at solving

It's all very well to educate your prospects, but don't forget that your goal is still to sell to them.

Your prospects have lots of problems that need solving, and it's important that you focus on the ones that you can solve better than anyone else.

3. Develop the problem before you sell the approach

Many inexperienced salespeople leap straight to the solution as soon as they hear their prospect has a problem they can solve. This is natural because they want to help the person, and they are excited about the sale. However, this is a massive mistake.

It's important that you explore the problem when you find it, develop it and, importantly, get agreement from the prospect that it's a problem that's worth solving.

4. Sell your approach before you sell your solution

Once you have developed the problem, it is common to jump into selling your solution. By doing this – by jumping straight to the features of your product – you commoditise your product or service and therefore cheapen it.

If you instead sell the best approach to the problem, you can develop credibility for it before even mentioning your product. When done well, this has the effect of getting the prospect to buy into and, importantly, believe in the best approach to the problem. By the time you get to your product or service, the decision is almost made.

5. Show why you're different before claiming you are better

Smart salespeople know that they need to show why their product is different before they can claim it is better. This is important, because prospects find it hard to distinguish between the different sellers' claims that their products are better, and they find these claims hard to remember.

What they will remember is what is distinctive about your product, because this is stored in a different part of the brain that is more accessible, as its content is of greater interest.

6. Enable the buyer to convince themselves

The result of an effective sale is that the prospect has convinced himself to buy your product or service; after all, he is the only one entitled to call anything a solution to his problem, because only he can determine whether the problem has actually been solved.

When you have effectively developed the problem, sold your approach and shown how you are different, it's a much smaller step for the prospect to invest in you, as it's the next logical choice.

Step 5: Deliver

A big mistake many businesses make is thinking that their job is done once the sale has been made. In fact, this is a critical time, as many customers experience buyer's remorse and there is still a high chance that the sale could fall through.

Delivery is dependent on three things:
1. Attention to detail
2. Communication
3. Remarkable Client Experience

It is of the utmost importance that you have systems in place to ensure that all details are taken care of ahead of time, that you communicate well with your customer, that you continue to validate your customer's decision to purchase from you, and that the post-sale service is exceptional.

This last point is very important, as customers don't always expect a remarkable experience after the purchase. This is a great opportunity to blow them away.

Step 6: Expand

You make a sale to gain a customer. Once a customer has purchased from you and you have delivered for the first time, your work is just beginning. This step is where you want to move from being a supplier to being a preferred partner. This massively increases the lifetime value of a customer.

You need two strategies:

1. Becoming a preferred partner – make them a preferred client

Stop thinking about being a preferred supplier and start thinking about how you can make them a preferred client; this is how to sell without selling.

The process is exactly the same as Develop, but your solution, when you demonstrate why you're different, must include a way for the customer to give you their business exclusively.

Remember the example I shared earlier about the 'agency race' in the medical recruitment industry? Because we got to understand the true needs of the client – that they needed solutions, not options – we created Preferred Client Relationships to deliver the solutions our clients needed. To do this, the hospitals had to remove themselves from the 'agency race'. They would send their vacancies to us 24 to 48 hours before releasing them to the market. We then had time to do our job and find each hospital the best-matched doctor, and so deliver to them a single solution. This saved the clients an average of 97 per cent on sourcing time, and it also saved them fees and increased quality.

As a result, we went from filling 14 per cent of their vacancies to 87 per cent of their vacancies, which happened over a two-month period.

It changed the game for our clients, and in doing that, it changed the game for my company.

And it was much better for the hospitals to want to be preferred clients rather than to make us their preferred supplier.

Remember, New Sales is all about the customer.

2. Remaining a preferred supplier

Remaining a preferred supplier is all about two things:

a. Consistent delivery of benefits: You have to stay in conversation with your clients to ensure that you continue to meet and exceed their evolving needs. Assume their needs will change and talk to them so that you can change with them. It is best to adapt to what they need before they know you need to adapt.

b. Communicate those benefits: Just because you're doing a great job, don't assume that your client is aware of all your benefits. It's your job to communicate in a way that the client can quickly see just how great it is doing business with you.

For our Preferred Client Relationships, we create monthly reporting that demonstrates the percentage of a client's vacancies we have filled and the monetary savings to them. We use these reports as a conversation starter to see how we could continue to better meet their needs and save them more money (by spending more with us).

SMALL-TICKET SALES: THE RAPID PERSUASION METHOD

The principles for small-ticket sales are exactly the same as for big-ticket sales, but the process has to happen a lot faster.

If you're selling a T-shirt, then investing a month in the sales process probably isn't wise. You need a powerful method that you can run in just a few minutes.

For products with shorter sales cycles, you need the Rapid Persuasion Method (RPM).

Step 1: Give them something

One of the easiest and most effective ways to influence someone is to give them something, because this engages the law of reciprocity.

Have you ever been at an airport and had a Hare Krishna come up to you and give you a flower, just because they 'wanted to'? They then ask you for a donation and, because you have accepted a gift from them, you feel compelled to give them something in return.

Testament to the law of reciprocity is that the Hare Krishnas get most of their flowers from the nearest rubbish bin, as the receiver didn't really want what they were given. However, because they accepted it, they feel obligated to give something back.

As humans we are hard-wired to avoid being in debt to someone.

A great way to start using RPM is by giving something to your customer. Generally it is something that costs you very little but would be perceived as valuable to them.

Possible things to give that cost you very little (or nothing):
- A genuine compliment.
- A comfy seat and a magazine for someone to take a rest.
- A chocolate or sweet.
- A coffee or a hot drink on a cold day.
- A cold drink on a hot day.
- An ear to listen.

The list is limitless, and a good question to help you figure out what you can give is: 'How can I show kindness to this person?'

This is not manipulation; this is showing kindness. Kindness just means that you are thinking about how you can add value to their day and make it a little better.

Step 2: Find out their logical needs

While people buy on emotion and justify with logic, it can seem confronting when you start too early to delve into people's emotional reasons for buying a product.

It's great to start by finding out their logical needs first, because this can be used as a prelude to discovering their emotional needs.

To determine their logical needs, you can just ask them what they are looking for. Chances are that they will share their logical needs – the features and benefits they are hoping to find.

Step 3: Find out their emotional needs

People come looking for a product or service, but what they are really looking for is an emotion.

Once you have uncovered the customer's logical needs, you can easily move on to uncovering their emotional needs.

Most salespeople never do this, and thus they are missing the key reason why a customer will buy something.

Some simple questions to draw out emotional needs are:
- Why do you want to buy that?
- If you got exactly what you wanted, how would it make you feel?

What's essential is that you don't project *your* emotional response to the product or the service onto the customer. No one cares how it would make *you* feel; this is about *them*.

Step 4: Align their needs with your product or service

Now that you know what they want, both logically and emotionally, your next step is to align what you're selling with those needs.

For example, if a customer wanted to buy a new ski jacket, your RPM conversation might have looked like this:

> **YOU:** *Nice work coming out shopping on this freezing day! We're only seeing the really hardy shoppers today. Can I offer you a hot chocolate to warm up?* (Step 1, **give** them something.)
>
> **CUSTOMER:** *Thanks, that would be lovely.*
>
> **YOU:** *How can I help you today?*
>
> **CUSTOMER:** *I'm looking for a new ski jacket.*
>
> **YOU:** *Excellent, I think we can probably help you. What do you need in a jacket?* (Step 2, find out their **logical needs**.)
>
> **CUSTOMER:** *I'm heading to France to ski, and it's going to be really cold, so I need a really warm and waterproof jacket.*
>
> **YOU:** *Great, we have lots of warm jackets, but tell me, how do you want to feel in this jacket?* (Step 3, find out their **emotional needs**.)
>
> **CUSTOMER:** *Well, I really like the way the US ski team look smart and fast at the same time – that's what I'm looking for.*

At this point, you know their logical and emotional needs, so it's time to align your product with those.

> **YOU:** *Here is a jacket that is actually made by the same people who supply the US ski team. It's comfortable and not too baggy, so it looks and feels fast, and as you can see it's beautifully made, so you feel really good wearing it.* (Step 4, **align with their needs**.)

This might seem really simple, but it's incredibly powerful and takes very little time.

Compare this with the usual approach of 'How can I help you?', then pointing someone to the jacket section of the store.

Step 5: Encourage visualisation

As I've said, the subconscious mind is estimated to be over 30 000 times more powerful than the conscious mind, and it thinks in images and emotions.

At this stage in RPM, you have started to engage the emotions; now it's time to add images.

This is as simple as asking someone to visualise themselves in a successful outcome with your product or service.

This might sound a bit weird, but it can be done in an elegant way that feels like a natural progression of the conversation. It must be delivered with confidence and enthusiasm to come across as genuine.

Remember, success is personal and it relates to the specific emotions and outcomes your customer wants.

In the case of the jacket sale, you might get them to put the jacket on, then say:

> **YOU:** *How does that feel? Can you see yourself ripping up the slopes, looking like you're in the US ski team, feeling fast, feeling smart, just feeling great? How do you like that?* (Step 5, **visualisation**.)

Step 6: Provide social proof

Another really powerful influencing technique is to provide social proof, showing a customer that others have achieved the exact results they want, so they don't feel alone.

In a sales situation, this is as simple as citing another person who got the exact same results that this customer wants. Be honest and don't belabour this step. If you don't have an example, then I don't think you should make one up. But if you can provide a real example, it's a great tool to help move someone over the line.

It might look like this:

> **YOU:** *You know, I had another customer in here the other day who wanted a jacket like the US ski team's, and I saw them yesterday and they were thrilled at just how great the jacket made them feel up the mountain. Isn't it amazing how something as simple as a great jacket can make you feel?* (Step 6, **provide social proof**.)

Step 7: Ask for the sale

It's amazing how many salespeople don't actually ask for the sale. If you've been through the RPM process successfully, then by now the customer is not only prepared to buy, they are excited about buying.

You now need to move them over the line.

You can just ask them if they would like to buy, or a great method is to assume the sale and just ask them how they want to pay for it. You have to work out what is natural for you.

> **YOU:** *Wow, you look good in that! How are you going to pay, cash or credit?* (Step 7, **ask for the sale**.)

At this point, if there are any objections, bring the person back to the emotion they want to feel by buying the jacket and get them to see themselves achieving exactly what they want to with your product or service.

Step 8: Expand

Once your customer has agreed to the sale, you have an opportunity to expand it.

A lot of people talk about 'up-selling', but that makes it all about you – selling more so that *you* make more.

And New Sales isn't about you. It's about the customer.

Expansion is different, because your focus is on helping your customer get even more of what they want with something else that you have.

It might sound very similar, but the intention is what matters.

In the case of the successful ski-jacket sale, expansion might look like this:

> **YOU:** *You know, if you really want to feel like you're in the US ski team, then have a look at these pants and goggles. I know for a fact that this is what they'll be wearing this winter, so you might enjoy them too.* (Step 8, **expand.**)

You are helping the customer to get more of what they want. You're being an effective salesperson. You're being a *good* salesperson.

New Sales is going to feel different from what you are doing now, so it's really important that you get comfortable with it. Practise it by yourself, then role-play with someone else. Do this until it feels pretty natural, then use it with customers. The more you use it, the better you will get and the more natural it will feel.

SIMPLIFYING SALES

As you can see from this chapter, a sale doesn't have to be manipulative and it doesn't have to be complicated. However, if you really want to simplify sales to its core essence, it comes down to being two things: enthusiastic and bold.

People love enthusiastic people. As you know, enthusiasm is contagious. If you are selling something and you're not enthusiastic, it doesn't matter what system you are following – chances are you aren't going to be very successful, because you will fail to get the customer excited. And an indifferent customer isn't likely to buy anything. If you're enthusiastic and following New Sales, you'll be unstoppable, but if you're *just* enthusiastic, then you are still better off than doing nothing.

Bold means being both courageous and compassionate; to sell effectively, you need to be both of these. You need to be courageous enough to engage with the customer, to be honest and to actually ask for the sale. And you need to be compassionate enough so that people know that you are looking out for their best interests, that you aren't trying to sell ice to an Eskimo!

SUMMARY

New Sales is simply about finding out what a customer wants, then giving them certainty that they will get that with your product or service.

The key to effective sales is to make it all about your customer; it's not about you at all. As soon as you start focusing on you, on your product or your service, then you join the masses and become extremely ineffective – and your customer will close up.

People open up and want to buy from you when you focus on them, on their needs, on their desires, on their problems, when you take the approach of solving their problems, and when you can genuinely align both your approach and your specific product or service with a solution your customer wants.

While your competition is pushing their product on your customers, you are like a breath of fresh air. With this process, you move across the table, sit beside your customer and approach the situation as their partner.

Your competition doesn't stand a chance, so they'll try harder, which makes them even more ineffective.

And that's just not fair.

That's the Unfair Fight.

ROUND 8

Culture and Team

A strong team is a formula for victory in any battle. If you don't have the right people, if they're not working together towards a common outcome, and if you haven't created an environment in which they can succeed, then the odds are stacked against you.

But when you do have great people working together towards a shared vision, then you tap into a massive power.

It is hard to master the art of the Unfair Fight by yourself. To use it in its full capacity you need leverage, meaning you extend the extent of your influence. That's exactly what a great team gives you.

I often get asked this question: 'What would you do differently if you had to start this business again?' I don't live with regrets, because everything that has happened has got me to where I am now, but I do believe that both success and failure leave clues so that we can learn from our mistakes.

One thing I'd do differently is that I'd hire talented people a lot quicker, and I'd be a lot more focused on creating an environment that they can thrive in rather than leaving that to chance.

The big corporates have departments to manage the hiring of people and still don't do a great job of it, and it's an area with which most small- and medium-sized business owners struggle and at which they do very badly. It is also one area that has a huge impact on whether you succeed or fail, and how enjoyable the journey is. Delegating is another area with which business owners often struggle, because they hold on to control for too long and become the neck of a funnel, stifling growth and success.

Most books on hiring and engaging people make it very complicated, so I'll demystify the process in this chapter and give you the keys to getting the best people, and then getting the best out of them.

The small- or medium-sized business owner can turn this weakness into a strength by applying some core principles that a corporate will never be able to do as effectively, because they are just too big.

Hiring and culture are where you can turn the Unfair Fight in your favour, by bringing together a group of people who can achieve the seemingly impossible.

Business owners need to be three things:

1. They need to be great talent scouts.
2. They need to have a vision that people can believe in.
3. They need to be able to create a culture in which their staff can thrive.

Employees are looking for this vision and passion in someone else, and as the business owner you need to provide it, and find people who buy into it.

I have realised that success in business is measured by what you can achieve for others. The success of a business owner can be judged by how well they can motivate their team. And the success of the team can be judged by how well they satisfy the customers.

This chapter is about how you can achieve these outcomes, for others and for yourself.

GROWTH TRAPS

There are six phases related to people and culture that businesses go through, often in order, to get to Optimal. By being aware of these phases, you can avoid the common traps. This section outlines the stages and the traps; how to avoid the traps is covered in the rest of the chapter. Awareness is key to avoiding or minimising the traps.

I have created this model based on original work by Keith Cunningham.

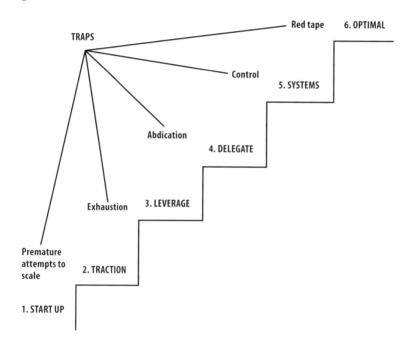

Most start-ups begin with a person, or people, and a creative idea. In the start-up phase it's important to do whatever it takes to gain traction to move to the next level, where you discover your niche. The trap many business owners fall into at this stage is trying to scale their business before they get traction. Scaling comes later – if you have a premature focus on scaling, your business will never get going.

Once you have traction, it's time to get leverage. You achieve this through other people. The trap at this point is to hold onto too much yourself and becoming exhausted. Many business owners can relate to this – they feel as if their business is running them, rather than them running their business.

In the traction phase, business owners will tell you that the customer is number one. As they gain leverage, they realise that while customers are important, it's employees who are number one. They realise the folly of putting customers before the very heart and soul of the business, the people who turn up every day and give their time towards the realisation of the vision.

Disinterested people deliver disinterested results, and the employee who feels like he or she comes second to the customer soon becomes disinterested.

When you have leverage, through your employees, it can be tempting to abdicate power, because it feels like you now have people to dump things on. This is a huge mistake – there is a massive difference between abdication and delegation, which is the next stage you want to reach. With delegation you remain accountable, with abdication you don't.

Once you are effectively delegating, it's time to focus on scale, on creating systems that mean you can consistently deliver great outcomes. The danger here is that the business owner tries to control every outcome and becomes a bottleneck. If you can get out of the way and be a part of creating effective systems, you move to the next level.

Once you have systems, there is a danger of overdoing it, of creating so much red tape that creativity gets stifled, and the great things that got your company to this point get lost. When you can ensure that you have effective systems without overdoing them, then you can move your company to Optimal.

This is another people-orientated way of looking at the stages of business growth. It is related to the life cycle of a business on page 24.

What can I, and only I, do in my business?

I have continuously asked myself this question. And the answer has evolved as my business has evolved.

Another way of thinking about this is to answer the question: 'What is the highest value use of my time right now?'

At the start of MedRecruit, when it was just Claire and me, the answer to the question was pretty much everything! We didn't have the capital to hire lots of people, so we had to put our heads down and do it all ourselves. As we grew and hired great people, the answer shifted to focus more and more on the core aspects to grow the business: vision, strategy and culture. When you're at this stage, a great question to ask is: 'What can someone else do better than me in my business?'

I don't believe in checking out of a business and getting it to run itself, as most business books will tell you to do. Checking out is a recipe for most businesses to fail spectacularly. I believe that it's important to stay engaged with any business you own, and at the same time to become more and more specialised in the areas that you, and only you, can do. By doing this, you and your business will evolve effectively.

BUSINESS SUCCESS

The scorecard of business success ultimately comes down to growth and profits. Customers are obviously critical to these outcomes, but underpinning everything you do is your employees.

This chapter is comprehensive, as it is essential to the Unfair

Fight, and while the lessons aren't complex, there are a number of things that must be addressed to get people and culture right. This is the biggest challenge facing most entrepreneurs and business owners, and it's standing between them and the success they desire.

CULTURE

Culture tells people how to think and act when you're not there. It is a way for people to quickly calibrate their behaviours to ensure that what is important happens consistently.

One of the main roles of the leader is to create and drive the culture of the organisation. This is not an area to delegate to your human resources department or office manager. I have learnt that the hard way. As Keith Cunningham says, culture is the biggest asset of any business; employees will come and go, but the culture remains and is enduring.

Culture is a reflection of leadership. A good culture is the sign of a good leader and, make no mistake, a bad culture is the sign of a bad leader.

Culture is like marriage – it needs to be nurtured. The key to a great culture is not starting it, it's maintaining it; realising that even when you have a great culture, you need to give it the love and attention it desires, just like you do with your partner.

THE GUIDERAILS

The Guiderails define the culture; they define the desired behaviours and the boundaries of what's acceptable. They tell your staff how to behave when you're not there. They are a combination of your core values and the ways those values need to be expressed. It is vital that your Guiderails are clearly communicated to the team – they can't be unspoken. The Guiderails help keep your team on track if they start to veer off course at any point.

The Guiderails show people both how to think and how to act to be successful.

An effective army knows exactly how they need to think and what they need to do to win the battle – your business is no different.

Hazledine Enterprises is my company that delivers resources such as this book and our online education content. Because it is so closely associated with me, it is important that we have extremely clear Guiderails so that I can be 100 per cent confident that only the best is delivered every time, in the way that I want it to be delivered. While most of the content comes from me, the delivery is equally as critical, and to ensure that this is exceptional, our people operate by these Guiderails.

Distinction
- Ensure what we deliver is unique
- Challenge the status quo

Excellence
- Constant and never-ending improvement
- Hunger to grow
- Go the extra mile
- Challenge people to grow and be their best

Caring
- Act with both heart and mind
- Solve real problems and make a meaningful difference
- Help people achieve their dreams
- Be generous – give more than we get

By clearly communicating these rules and making them part of a daily, ongoing dialogue, they have become part of Hazledine Enterprise's

DNA. This is what my business is about, and everyone knows how to behave accordingly.

Create your own Guiderails with this exercise:
1. Get your team together without any distractions. This is important and warrants their full attention.
2. Talk about the customer experience – what do they want? Ensure that your people, and not just you, are coming up with the answers, so that they buy into the process.
3. Talk about the team experience – what do they want? Your people are the lifeblood of your business, so the culture must serve them. This will ensure that they buy into the process.
4. Brainstorm behaviours and beliefs that would create a horrible customer experience, and a horrible employee experience. People often have a lot of fun with this and come up with some real shockers.
5. Brainstorm what would create the desired experience for both customers and employees.
6. Group the beliefs and behaviours that you do want into common categories. You are looking not just for what people said, but for the reason they said it, the essence of it.
7. Condense it down to a maximum of five values; three is optimal.
8. Map out what it means to live each of these values.

You now have your Guiderails – share these with everyone, hire and fire based on them, and encourage them in every aspect of your business.

Access the full Guiderails exercise by registering at www.samhazledine.com.

VISION

The vision of a business is very important in helping to determine the culture. While many corporations have long and theatrical visions, I am yet to meet a CEO who knows by heart one of these kinds of vision. And if the CEO doesn't know it, how can she expect her employees to know it and live it?

The vision has to be short, it has to be memorable, and it has to cut to the heart of what the business is all about – the 'why'. This is covered in detail in Round 2 (see page 64).

At MedRecruit, the vision is to 'Enrich Lives': the lives of our doctors, of the hospitals, of the patients, of our staff, and of anyone we come into contact with.

Everyone in the company knows this simple vision, which drives our culture.

Think about your reason for being in business and why you got into business, what impact you want to have, and distil this into your vision.

DRIVING QUESTION

People think in questions, so a great way to direct your focus is to ask a great question. A brilliant way to simplify culture for your staff is to create a Driving Question that keeps their focus in alignment with the culture.

At MedRecruit, our Driving Question is: 'What more can I do?'

Team members ask this consistently and it helps guide their behaviour moment by moment.

The key to creating your Driving Question is to ask yourself what your team needs to focus on to deliver at the highest level for your customers. Then find the question that best answers this focus.

This process is covered in detail in Round 12. For now, just keep in mind that it's something that will massively benefit your business.

TEAM

The point of having a culture is to provide a framework for your team to perform in the way they need to. And for a culture to be effective, you need the right people in your team. A great culture will come unstuck with the wrong people, and great people can come unstuck with a bad culture. With the culture defined and in place, you have what you need to hire the right people, set them up for success and, when needed, let them go.

As a business owner you need to become very good at all three of these aspects of creating a great team.

HIRING

My simple rule of thumb is to hire people who are better than me in different areas of the business. I once hired a manager who I knew had less experience and talent than me because I thought I could mould him into a mini-me. This was a huge mistake, because that area of the business suffered as soon as I let go of it, and it didn't improve and grow until that person was moved on and I hired someone with a lot more experience and expertise than me.

Who do you need?

Most business books tell you to create an organisational chart in the image of the company you want to create. This can be the kiss of death when it comes to hiring people, because it means business owners fail to focus on what's really important – producing results.

I recommend that you start with the results that you are looking to achieve. Then look at the person you need to deliver these results, and what specific skills, experience and behaviours will get the job done. Consider this along with your culture and look for people who will add to the culture, not detract from it.

While this seems really basic and obvious, I often see people start with an organisational chart, which doesn't work.

Where to find the talent

Once you know exactly who you need, the next stage of hiring is to identify potential talent. There are a number of great places to source people, and these will vary for different industries, but in my experience, and in order of effectiveness, these are the best:

1. Existing employees

Other than you, no one knows your business and its needs like your employees. Generally speaking, your employees care about their reputation too, so when they suggest someone for a position, you should get very excited. Generously reward your employees for referring good people.

2. The competition

Find people with a demonstrated competence in your field who might be dissatisfied with the culture of the company they are working for and are looking for a better option. By focusing on having a great culture you can make your business very attractive to people already in your industry. It's a great position to be in when they are coming to you rather than you going to them.

3. Suppliers and customers

You have an insight into how these people work that you won't get in a job interview. This is one of the best ways of knowing how they'll perform in your company.

4. Recruiters

Some positions can be harder to recruit for than others, and may be costing you money for every day they aren't filled. In these instances, getting a professional recruiter involved is a great way to source talent.

5. *Online, newspapers, etcetera*

Local papers are a good way to source staff, as are internet job boards, when you want to cast the net a bit wider.

The six common hiring mistakes

Once you've found the talent, you need to go through a hiring process. Most people make an absolute mess of this stage, which is why they are so bad at hiring good employees.

Here are the six common hiring mistakes and how to avoid them:

1. *Lack of clarity*

When you hire someone based on the organisational chart that the last business book told you to create, you'll end up with the wrong person and a 'fat' company.

The first thing you must do when it comes to hiring people is to get absolute clarity about who you need.

As I said above, you have to get clear on the results they need to deliver, who they need to be and how they need to act to achieve those results.

Second, you need to get clear on the personality you are looking for. When you do this, you can quickly assess a person's potential suitability and you won't compromise on who you need.

Make a list of the 'must-have' traits, a list of the 'nice-to-have' traits, and also a list of the 'must-not-have' traits.

You now have a scorecard with which to rank people.

For example, when I hire business-development people, the one trait they must have is immediate likeability – if they don't, then I quickly rule them out for this role, which saves both of us a lot of time.

2. *Interviewing poorly*

You need to ensure that you are buying, not selling, in an interview. Don't fall into the trap of trying to convince the candidate to choose you. Make sure they are selling themselves to you and make sure you are interviewing them, as opposed to *them* interviewing *you*.

Most interviews are a chat, and the chat is flexible and therefore usually different between different candidates, so you don't end up comparing apples with apples. You need two effective interviews; the first interview is to screen people to decide whether to progress them to the second interview, where you really dive deep.

Here are five questions I learnt from Keith Cunningham that you can use to keep Interview One focused and relevant:

1. What do you know about us?

This will indicate whether a candidate had the initiative to do some research on your company. If they haven't even bothered to do this, or if they really don't understand you, then rule them out. I was interviewing a candidate recently who takes the cake for the worst answer to this question. Initially, she said, 'MedRecruit, right?' to confirm whom she was talking to. That's an immediate red flag that she was playing a broad field. Then she said, 'Well, the name "MedRecruit" implies you're in medicine and in recruitment.' She hadn't done any research and was simply telling me what our name implied. Next!

2. What five things do you love to do at work?

Ask someone what they are good at and they'll tell you what they *think* you want to hear, but ask them what they love and they'll tell you what they're good at without realising it.

3. What five things do you hate to do at work?

As with asking what someone loves, asking what someone doesn't enjoy will tell you what they aren't very good at.

4. What do you think are the five most important things for you to be successful in this job?

This is a great question to see if they really understand what it's going to take to be great at the role. It also gives you an insight into their values, which is critical to see if they align with your culture.

5. What are some things your current employer can do to be more successful?

This will tell you if they can see opportunities and if they are going to bring insight, creativity and innovation to your business.

Download the Interview Questionnaire by registering at www.samhazledine.com.

Interview One will give you an overview of the person so that you can make a quick comparison between candidates to decide whether to move them to Interview Two, where you invest some serious time.

Interview Two is a chronological, in-depth interview, which is the best way to give you strong insights into people's strengths and weaknesses, and any limitations related to the scorecard you developed when you scoped the role. It lasts one to two hours, compared with the first half-hour chat, and it covers the candidate's entire career history in detail. It does not rely on hypothetical questions that are easy to make up answers to, but instead focuses on their real experiences.

This type of interview format makes it easy to spot patterns and identify people's strengths and weaknesses.

For each job or role in a person's career, ask about:

- The expectations they had of that role.
- Their responsibilities in that role.
- Their accomplishments.
- Any failures or areas in which they weren't as successful as they'd have liked.
- What their supervisor would say were their strengths and weaknesses in that role.
- Their reasons for leaving.

Years of research have shown that this is the best process to provide an accurate assessment of people, far better than informal interviews and even workplace suitability testing.

3. Missing critical hiring steps

Hiring people can make or break your business. So don't take short cuts, because you will get burnt. In my experience, this order must be followed:

CV and cover-letter review: Quickly rule out the people who aren't suitable, and decide who deserves an interview. In the job advertisement I also ask them to call and leave a message, answering some simple questions. It's amazing how many people can't follow this two-step process, and if they can't do that, I don't want them.

Interview One: The screening interview where you ask the five questions to see if candidates are potential options or not – this is a quick interview, as you will have a number of people to speak with.

Interview Two: This is your chance to delve deep in a chronological, in-depth interview. You can also give people role-plays and challenges to see how they actually perform. I find this much more accurate than the personality testing many HR people like to use.

References: Always get at least three references to check on any areas of concern from the previous three steps. And while some candidates might resist giving you their current employer as a reference, I insist on this as the final check before hiring someone. My advice is to never hire someone without talking to their current employer, or if they aren't working, then their last employer. If they aren't forthcoming, they are usually hiding something, which is a good reason to avoid hiring them.

4. Hire people like us

The best reason for hiring people is to bring something to the business that you don't have. It is crucial to remember that you are looking for different skills, behaviours, talents and perspectives. You want people who are better, faster, more methodical, more analytical, more intuitive, and so on. For example, when I hire a CFO, I want them to consider the downside risk of things more than I do – I've got more than enough optimism, and I need people to ask me the tough questions.

Don't mistake this for hiring people who don't fit the culture; while you want different kinds of people in the business, everyone must buy into the culture and be pulling in the same direction as a team.

5. Hire too fast

By now you should be getting the idea that hiring people is essential to your success and that the process can't be rushed. Make sure that you don't fall into the trap of just getting a bum on a seat, rather than finding the right talent to support your business's growth. The cost of making a mistake is much higher than you think, because it includes the direct costs of hiring, training and replacing, and the much bigger, indirect cost of what you missed out on by getting the wrong person. The costs of replacing staff range from 100 per cent to 400 per cent of an annual salary, so don't rush it and get it wrong.

6. Employ, don't engage

If you avoid the first five mistakes but don't pay enough attention to your culture, then your initially motivated new employees will become disgruntled, lose interest and go off the boil.

When, and only when, you move from employing people to engaging them in a supportive environment, then, and only then, will you have a team who is committed and able to deliver on the vision of your company.

HIGH PERFORMANCE

Business owners generally hold on too long by themselves before taking on new staff, but when they do, they make the equally stupid mistake of abdicating their success to others.

Delegation is very different from abdication.

With delegation there is the transfer of responsibility, but there is also the expectation that you will verify that what you want done actually happens. As the leader of a business, you remain accountable for its success.

With abdication, you essentially wash your hands of a task and you relinquish accountability for the success of your business. This is a bad idea, because not only are you likely to be the one who cares most about your business, but if your staff see you as disinterested, they are less likely to do a good job, so it's a double-edged sword.

Stay engaged, verify what your team is doing, and expect the best.

Caring

A high-performance culture must be underpinned by a culture of caring. When your employees know they are cared about, they will demand more of themselves than you could ever demand, and they will strive for high performance. When you create a culture of caring, all you need to do is provide the framework for them to deliver on high performance; you don't have to spend all your time motivating your staff.

Caring starts with an attitude, and is expressed with actions. It is important that you genuinely appreciate your employees and are committed to their best outcomes. They will feel this.

There are so many actions you can take to show you care. Here are a few examples:

- Say ,'Thank you, I appreciate you.'
- Write them a personal card.
- Spend time with them – ask them about their jobs and how you can support them.
- Show a real interest in their personal lives.
- Remember their birthdays.
- Make time for the team to socialise outside of work.
- Provide resources for your team to develop personally and professionally.
- Align their personal goals with the company goals so that they can achieve what they want by being part of your company.
- Provide benefits such as:
  - Time during the day to exercise.
  - Fresh fruit in the office.
  - An extra day of leave for every year they work for you.

As you can see, caring is primarily an attitude, and it doesn't have to be expensive. There are so many things you can do. I start by listening to my team so that I understand what they want, then I provide what is feasible. It's like differentiating your business – find out what they want, go out and get it, and give it to them.

REMUNERATION

While it'd be nice if your staff worked for you out of the kindness of their hearts, the reality is that remuneration is critical.

I think it's a great idea, if you can, to pay people enough to take money off the negotiation table, so that it is not an issue.

For different roles there will be a mix of base salary and perhaps a performance bonus. I think it's advantageous if all staff can have some influence on what they earn, and my rule of thumb is to only give people performance bonuses on the things they can directly influence.

For example, my sales manager is incentivised on the sales that are made, not on profit. The reason for this is because they have a direct influence on sales, but there are many factors outside their control that influence profits. On the other hand, my chief operating officer does earn bonuses based on profit, because he has a direct influence on the many factors that influence profit.

Giving people equity is something a lot of employees want, but this should be entered into very carefully and only be given to people whose services you can't pay for. My general rules for people who have equity in my businesses are:

- Don't do it if you can avoid it.
- Really, if you can avoid it, then don't do it.
- Seriously, avoid it if you can!
- They need to earn it – don't give anything away for free.
- It is preferable to vest the equity over time – don't give it all up front, because the incentive to do a great job gets lost.
- Set up the shareholder agreement before handing over equity,

and set it up so that if they aren't performing, you can let them go without protracted negotiations.

- If people want to share in the upside, they must also share in any downside.

Even if the business is not in a position to pay more, reviews should occur on a regular basis. If the business is in a position to improve pay, then this should be done primarily on performance, not on longevity.

COACHING BELIEFS VERSUS MANAGING BEHAVIOURS

When business owners aren't getting the results they want from their employees, they tend to focus on the employees' performance – what they're doing. This seems logical, but it rarely delivers long-term and lasting results.

A powerful distinction I learnt from Keith Cunningham is that the results employees deliver come from the actions they take, which come from the behaviours they engage in, which are driven by their beliefs. Coaching the beliefs that underpin the behaviours that lead to the actions that deliver the results is the most effective way to bring about real and lasting change.

RESULTS

↑

ACTIONS

↑

BEHAVIOURS

↑

BELIEFS

For example, if an employee consistently misses deadlines, you could focus on tasks like time management to get the job done. But if you go deeper and ask them a question along the lines of: 'For you to consistently not meet deadlines you must believe that it's okay to not keep your word and to let yourself down, let the rest of the team down, and let me down. Is this true?' You'll find that in almost all cases your employee doesn't believe this. By shining light on their behaviour and what it means to others, their belief instantly changes, which changes their behaviour and their actions – and therefore the results.

And another benefit of this is that the employee often improves across a number of areas, not just the one you are coaching on.

If the employee does believe in that behaviour, then don't lower your expectations. It's time to move them on.

This is the single most powerful tool I have found for empowering people to massively improve.

LEADERSHIP

High performance requires strong and effective leadership. And while countless books have been written on 'leadership', I think it essentially comes down to setting the focus for the organisation and creating a culture for people to thrive in. Employees will look to the leaders to tell them what's important and where to focus, so the leaders must be disciplined in where they focus their own, and their people's, energies.

Round 4 covered this in a lot more detail (see page 95).

MISTAKES

If you haven't made one of the six common hiring mistakes, and someone in your business isn't performing, then usually it's due to unmet expectations – either yours or your employee's.

I believe that if someone is telling you who they are, believe them.

It's not my job to care more about their job than them, so sometimes it's important to let people go and move on.

GETTING BACK ON TRACK

I used to struggle a lot with how to manage underperformance, because I couldn't define it. Then Keith Cunningham taught me a concept that now defines how I operate: coach cultural issues, and train performance issues. It is important that you see ongoing cultural fit as just as critical as job performance – in fact, I think it's *more* important. It's the person who is great at their job but really undermines the culture who is the most dangerous person to your company. It is these people who need a very public hanging, as this sends the message loud and clear that you aren't just a company that talks about culture, you actually live and die by it.

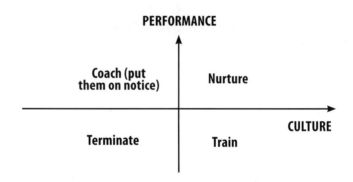

When you do let someone go, tell them it isn't because they're a bad person, it's just that they weren't the right fit for your business. I have never had to fire someone who I genuinely didn't think would be better off working elsewhere.

People generally welcome coaching and effective training, which is telling them what's wrong and also how to improve it, while people often don't like feedback, which is just telling them what's wrong. It should not come as a surprise to anyone that the first place to start when someone is underperforming is with either coaching or training.

MANAGING YOUR PEOPLE
Your team needs both leadership and management, and the two are quite different.

Leadership has been covered in Round 4. Management is something that can be made incredibly difficult, or it can be made simple.

The challenge is to stick with it and to not lose interest. This is a danger for those entrepreneurs who are too busy focusing on the 'next big thing' to manage their people effectively.

SETTING YOUR PEOPLE UP FOR SUCCESS

Define the target

↓

Clarify the projects and tasks

↓

Assign responsibility and communicate expectations

↓

Stay engaged

But the reality is that unless people are really clear on what it takes to be successful, it's hard for them to stay on track, to stay motivated and to make the biggest contribution to the organisation that they can.

1. Define the target

Be 100 per cent clear on the target: what you are striving to achieve. While this seems obvious, it's amazing how many business owners aren't clear on it, and how even more employees aren't clear on it either.

If you're going on a trip, you need to know the destination; start with this.

2. Clarify projects and tasks

Once you know *where* you are going, you need to know *how* you are getting there. Determine the projects and clarify the individual tasks within these projects. This is essentially like determining the route on the map that will get you to your desired destination.

3. Assign responsibility and communicate expectations

Once you are clear on where you are going and how you are going to get there, it's time to assign responsibility for each step and to communicate your expectations.

People love clarity, so this step spells out exactly how they can be successful in their role. If you've hired correctly, then this is exactly what your people want. If they don't want clarity and responsibility, you've got the wrong people.

Communicate the tasks, the levels of quality, the timelines, the check-in points and the results that are needed. Take time with this, because the more time spent doing this, the less time you'll spend correcting people.

4. Stay engaged

It's tempting at this point to check out and let your people get on with it. But disinterested managers do not get the best from their teams.

Check in when you said you'd check in. Don't just give things a cursory look, be interested and ensure that things are moving in the right direction. A successful business has a lot of moving parts and often the only person with an overview of everything is the business owner, or the business leader, so it's critical that you are looking at how everything is unfolding and coming together so that you get a coordinated effort from your team.

A vital part of ensuring that your managers take ownership of the strategic objectives of their departments is to get them to contribute to the action plans. By creating the plans themselves, these talented people are not only empowered, but they are also saying what they will do, so by definition the objectives are agreed upon and they have total buy-in.

It is important that you are available and involved in making these plans; this is delegation, not abdication. By the end of this process, you will have a plan that you all agree upon and that everyone is committed to putting into action.

SUMMARY

If you really care about your company and you care about delivering real results, then you have to call it tight in all areas of your business, especially when it comes to your people.

It's not caring to let things slide, it's not caring to tolerate mediocrity and it's not caring to let anyone undermine the culture.

Culture is the litmus test of leadership and leaders must be courageous in defending it; remember that culture is your business's greatest asset.

Excellence is a relentless commitment to focusing on what matters, and exceptions really are the enemy of excellence. Engaged employees are key to leveraging a business to achieve its potential.

Creating a high-performance culture involves bringing in the right people, providing fair and accurate assessment of performance, setting your people up so that they know how to succeed and staying engaged to ensure that they do succeed.

Your competition can't compete with a strong, unified and effective team who is focused on its core drivers of success.

It's just not fair – on the competition.

That's winning the Unfair Fight.

ROUND 9

Planning for Results

Most business owners struggle to translate what they have learnt into a workable plan that can be turned into meaningful results.

With the Unfair Fight you have the information and strategies you need to transcend your competition and to make your business a massive success.

Now you need a plan to translate what you've learnt into results.

There are a lot of misconceptions about business planning, so let's get clear on what you are trying to achieve here.

An effective business plan gives you the most focused and direct route to overcome a worthy challenge and to get you from where you are to where you want to go. Your plan has the ability to measure and refine your progress. Your plan is about achieving results with the least hassle.

That's it.

A business plan is not a massive document that gets prepared each year because you think you need one and then is never looked at again because it is so complex that it gives you a headache just thinking about it. But this is what most business plans look like, so many business owners get disillusioned and start operating with no plan.

This is the beginning of the decline in any business. It's like a pilot taking off and heading out over the ocean in any direction, hoping they'll get somewhere they like before they run out of fuel. They might land in Hawaii, but they're more likely to crash and burn.

The key to an effective plan is to ensure that it is fuelled by your vision, that it solves worthy challenges, and that it is built with a governing approach and actions that must be taken.

To have an effective plan, you also need to gain agreement from your team on what you are trying to achieve, and to ensure that the company and your people are willing and prepared to act on the plan once it is adopted.

By mastering Round 9 you become part of the small percentage of businesses that aim directly at their target, and you leave your competition zig-zagging their way to mediocrity.

The Unfair Fight is like you racing your competition from A to B when your course is in a straight line and theirs is the scenic route.

BEFORE YOU BEGIN PLANNING FOR RESULTS

The purpose of your plan is to achieve results quickly and efficiently. To have an effective plan you need to have completed some important steps from earlier chapters:

Vision that inspires – Round 2

You need to be clear on the ultimate aim for your company. See page 64.

Mission that moves – Round 2

You need to know what business you are really in – the emotion your customers either knowingly or unknowingly want from you. This will drive everything you do. See page 66.

Differentiation strategy – Round 5

It is important that you are clear on how you are going to differentiate your business; whether you have decided to create an entirely new category, to become the authority in your category, or to become the best in your category. See page 111.

As you create your plan, you will also want to review whether your differentiation strategy is appropriate and whether it will deliver the desired results.

PLANNING FOR GROWTH

Top-line growth is critical for any company just to stay alive. In business, as in life, you are either growing or you're dying. Remember that study by McKinsey & Company that showed companies that grow slower than GDP are five times more likely to fail than companies that outgrow GDP?

Growing your business goes beyond looking at industry averages to making decisions about where to focus your energy so that you can outgrow the average. This is particularly important in 'mature' markets, which don't show much growth. However, within these markets there are always high-growth areas where you can outperform the average.

There are always businesses beating the odds, and there are actually not that many ways to do so.

Three ways to grow

There are three main ways you can grow your company:

1. *Market segment momentum*

This is organic revenue growth achieved through the different market segments you operate in. You can influence this in several ways: you can select faster-growing market segments, you can select acquisitions in higher-growth segments, you can divest in the slower-growth segments, and you can create market growth by introducing a new product or service category to the market.

2. Merger and acquisition
You can buy or sell revenues through acquiring or merging with companies in different market segments.

3. Market share
You can gain or lose market share through your company's performance.

Of these three growth strategies, most businesses focus on gaining market share. And this is where you can come unstuck.

That same study by McKinsey & Company found that market segment momentum accounted for most growth (2 to 18 per cent per annum), mergers and acquisitions accounted for the second most growth (-1 to 13 per cent), and market-share performance accounted for the least growth (-6 to 5 per cent).

So while gaining market share seems to be the most obvious strategy for most businesses, it is often more effective and easier to grow your business by focusing on specific market segments that are performing well, or through acquiring other businesses in the growth segments you are interested in.

Figuring out the growth segments of your market is actually easier than you might think. The first way is to analyse your own sales data to see what regions and segments are doing best. Then, instead of putting most of your energy into improving the lower-performing areas, as most businesses do, you can focus your energy on the high-growth areas that are doing well – these are likely to give you a much better return.

The second way is to get external market data. This is often available from the annual reports of publicly listed companies, and Google is a great tool to find this sort of data, too.

For any business, gaining market share is also very achievable *if* you have a compelling business-model advantage. The thing is that most businesses don't have this, so they try to get more market share through superior execution, which is not effective.

Winning the Unfair Fight has given you many ways to create a compelling business-model advantage that will elevate you above your competition in the eyes of your customers, so by combining that with a focus on the high-growth market segments in your industry, you can accelerate growth and beat the average.

Seeking growth is rarely about changing industries, which is a risky proposition for most companies. It is about prioritising time and resources on the faster-growing segments of your market where you already have the capabilities, assets and insights that are needed for profitable growth, and creating a compelling business-model advantage.

This is important to keep in mind as you develop your plan.

Make sure you are planning for growth, because that's necessary just to stay alive.

WHAT DO YOU NEED?

Before you begin planning, you need to decide whether you want to transcend your competition or compete head to head. When it comes to transcending the competition, there are two important areas you can concentrate on: 'game-changers' and 'incremental improvements'.

Planning is about choosing where to focus and when. Your business needs a framework to help you focus your attention and action. This bottom-up process culminates in you achieving your ultimate outcome for your business and transcending your competition.

Most people focus on the top and what they ultimately want their business to be. It's great to keep this in mind, but the problem with this approach is that you can become overwhelmed by this huge outcome when you don't have a framework to achieve it.

What follows is the framework that can make you the market leader in any industry.

Identifying a worthy challenge

The problem with most strategic planning is that it focuses on what you want, rather than what you are being called for. This will be covered in more detail later in this chapter, but for now understand that the worthy challenge is the foundation of all effective strategy.

To become the market leader, to transcend the big guys, you need to understand what's needed, not just what you want.

'Game-changers' versus 'incremental improvements'

Once you have identified a worthy challenge, you can come up with ways to overcome it. Your ideas can fall into two categories: those that will make gradual progress, and those that will make massive progress towards transcending your competition and achieving your ultimate outcome.

Game-changers are ideas and innovations that leapfrog the competition. Generally, these are things that have the potential to revolutionise the way your industry does business. These are the big innovations that take time to develop and don't come along every day.

Incremental improvements are the constant and never-ending improvements and adjustments that you make on a daily basis to improve your business.

To transcend competition, you need both. If you just focus on game-changers, your daily business can suffer and you'll lose customers; if you just focus on incremental improvements, you get caught up in what is and lose sight of what could be.

The two are integrally linked, however, because by making incremental improvements and making constant progress, as long as you are looking, you will identify opportunities and obstacles that could become game-changers.

Execution or strategy?

You need a limited number of game-changers and a lot of incremental improvements to create a great business and to transcend your competition.

Some people have a propensity to always be looking for the game-changers; they are only excited if they are rebuilding their company or making massive changes. There's a danger to this, because the reality is that there aren't that many actual game-changers. These people can mistake activity for progress, and while they only have eyes for game-changers, they forget about making their business really great by making incremental improvements.

Some people get so focused on the gradual improvements that they fail to raise their heads to see what their industry might be calling out for, and then their competition implements a game-changer that makes them obsolete.

You need to get the balance right in your business.

Generally, you will have one to a maximum of three game-changers that you are working on at any particular time. If you have already identified your game-changers, you just need to focus on their execution, so that these strategies do actually change the game.

If you have no game-changers and you are just making incremental improvements, you are probably much more immersed in execution. But if you also want to improve exponentially, you need to start thinking strategically and actively looking for your game-changer.

Transcending the competition

Transcending the competition is an outcome, not an action. By identifying a worthy challenge to overcome, by using both game-changers and incremental improvements in an optimal balance, thereby balancing strategy and execution, you will ultimately transcend the competition.

And you just might become the market leader.

STRATEGY AND TACTICS

Often the terms *strategy* and *tactics* are used interchangeably and in a haphazard manner that confuses business owners.

Put simply, strategy is what drives the business direction; tactics are how those outcomes are achieved.

But for the purposes of creating a plan that is going to drive results, which is really what this is all about, you need both a direction and the actions to take; they can't be considered separately, as one determines the other.

So from this point on we will look at these two concepts together and call it 'Planning for Results', and it will become extremely clear how they interrelate.

PLANNING FOR RESULTS

Identify a worthy challenge

↓

Decide on your governing approach

↓

Determine the action steps

↓

Measure and correct

Define a worthy challenge

As I mentioned before, the problem with most business planning is that it starts with what *you* want, with setting goals. But, as I've covered time and again in this book, the market doesn't care what you want. You exist to provide for the market, not the other way round.

The fact that planning starts with identifying a worthy challenge is by design; how you *define* the challenge will determine the entire plan, it's that important.

The challenges facing every business are complex, convoluted and extremely broad – that's simply the reality. In effectively defining the worthy challenge, you should take this complexity and then identify factors that are critical. Frame it in a way that is simple to understand and communicate, and define it in a way that you can solve it. It is not until this is done that you can then address the challenge in a coherent manner. If the challenge facing you remains complex, your response is likely to be shotgun and ineffective. With a well-defined challenge, your response can be sniper-accurate and infinitely more effective.

I will not share any current personal examples here, because effectively defining the worthy challenge is the core of my entire business, and this is one thing that I don't want my competition to know. But I will share an example from when I started MedRecruit.

At the time, back in 2006, I noticed that 25 per cent of junior doctors were leaving medicine within three years of graduation. From talking to them I could see that the issue was that the medical profession hadn't evolved to meet the needs of the new generation of doctors, so they were becoming disillusioned and leaving. Essentially, I framed the worthy challenge as: the medical profession hasn't evolved to meet the lifestyle needs of Generation Y doctors.

Here are some ways to help you define the challenge that you face:

1. Pick a core challenge

Given the almost infinite number of challenges facing every business, it's tempting to list multiple challenges that you want to overcome. The problem with this is that it doesn't focus your actions and therefore doesn't give you any advantage. A business is most effective with a single point of focus, so it's important to make decisions and to stratify challenges to come up with the 'worthy' challenge: the one core challenge that really needs solving. This one skill will differentiate the successful businessperson from the unsuccessful one.

2. Focus on a challenge that you can solve

There's no point defining a challenge in such a way that it becomes impossible to overcome. For example, if I defined a challenge for MedRecruit as 'a core dissatisfaction in the medical profession', then that would be something that I can't overcome. You must define a problem in a way that allows you to develop an approach to solving it, or it's a pointless exercise.

3. External challenges

Often a worthy challenge will be a challenge that exists in the market from the perspective of your customers. It might look like a need that isn't being met, like a problem that isn't being effectively solved, or a change in buyer behaviour.

4. Internal challenges

Sometimes the challenge isn't actually in the marketplace; sometimes it's an internal challenge that your business faces that would make the biggest difference if you overcame it. For example, if you are operating in a healthy, growing market but your culture is one of laziness and entitlement, then focusing externally will not benefit your business. Unless you address the *real* worthy challenge of your company's culture, you will fail to get the go-forward you need.

5. Data and intuition

This is not a diagnosis; it's a hypothesis – an educated guess.

When identifying the worthy challenge, you are going to want to gather as much data as you can to support your hypothesis. However, data alone is not going to reveal the challenge; you are going to have to use your judgement and intuition to make a decision.

Essentially, you need to find just enough dots so that you can connect them to form a picture.

Remember, how you define the worthy challenge will determine your entire plan, so spend the time on this that it warrants.

Decide on your governing approach

Your Governing Approach is the overall, descriptive method with which you will overcome the worthy challenge. It is the way you are going to act to overcome the challenge and the limits you choose to operate within.

A key to deciding on your Governing Approach is to look for sources of advantage that you have, on things that you can leverage, to create the greatest response to your actions.

In the case of MedRecruit, the Governing Approach I chose was: Align as one of them and provide a great lifestyle for junior doctors within the current medical system. With this as our Governing Approach, we became the fastest-growing service business in the country.

There are many ways to find your sources of advantage:

1. How can you increase value in ways your competition can't?
What can you do to add value for your customers that would be extremely hard, or not cost-effective, for your competition to imitate? Is there information you have that they can't access? Are there systems that provide a speed or accuracy advantage that they don't have? Look for ways in which you can make a meaningful difference to the lives of your customers that are not easily copied.

2. How can you reduce cost in ways your competition can't?
Are there cost savings that you can make that would not be possible for your competition? What are the creative ways in which you could reduce costs while increasing quality, rather than reducing it? Most people associate reducing costs with reducing quality, so it takes some serious thinking and a creative mind to come up with a Governing Approach that reduces costs and increases quality at the same time.

3. How can you strengthen protective mechanisms that block imitation?
The most common ways to protect a competitive advantage are with patents and trademarks. But these are not the only way.

If you practise effective innovation, as mentioned earlier in the book, then you are able to present a moving target that the imitators never catch up to. This requires a rigorous commitment to constant innovation; it's not the path of least resistance, so most people shy away from it.

Determine the action steps

Your Governing Approach sets the overall approach, and the limits you place upon your business to keep you focused; the action steps are the specific actions that will make your Governing Approach a reality.

The reason you have created a Governing Approach is to prioritise the actions you want to take. There are a million things you can do in your business, but your Governing Approach acts like a filter to help you decide on what you will do to address the worthy challenge.

Your action steps take into account three frameworks:

The Strategic Framework

This is how you are going to structure your solution. It takes into account the resources you have available to achieve the tasks you have chosen. To pull this off, consideration must also be given to the market you are operating in, the stage it is at in its life cycle, other, external influences, and your core competencies. Ensure that your plan considers the consequences of the actions taken and mitigates for these. Work towards specific deadlines.

The People Framework

Consider the capabilities you need and whether you have these on your team or not. You can then decide who else you might need to add to the team or what training may be required, or who is surplus to the project. Make sure that the culture you have in your business is conducive to reaching the target, because the best plan can come completely unstuck if the culture doesn't support it.

The Operations Framework

The project will succeed or fail based on your execution. Ensure that ownership and responsibilities are crystal clear, determine the behaviours and tasks that are necessary, and make sure that the consequences are spelt out.

These frameworks are expanded upon in Round 10, which is 100 per cent devoted to execution.

Measure and correct

For any plan to be effective, it is important at the beginning to identify what you are going to measure to determine whether you are moving in the right direction and whether you are ultimately successful. It is also important to determine when these measurements will take place, how the data will be collected, who will be collecting the data and what you will do with the data.

This bit is not rocket science, but it is often neglected, and without it you can't know whether you are moving towards El Dorado or Niagara Falls!

I was recently doing a talk to a group of bookstore owners. As I usually do when I'm presenting, I asked the person organising the event if there was anything specific he wanted me to cover. His response was, 'Among other things, could you please spend some time talking with us about the current state of our retail industry, books and stationery, which are, particularly in the case of books, in the decline stage and see if we can come up with ideas on how we might start reversing some trends in our stores?'

He wanted me to help solve the challenge of consumers shifting their buying behaviour to online – just a small challenge to solve in the hour!

We started with identifying the worthy challenge. The tendency from the participants was to jump to things like declining sales, not enough foot traffic, increasing cash flow – things that were either symptoms they were experiencing or wishes they had. This is common for business owners. They set strategy by what they want, not what they are being called to do. I kept redirecting, and we ended up with a list of potential challenges:

- Consumers moving purchasing online and overseas.
- More supply channels to compete with.
- Local bookstores aren't as convenient as online purchasing.
- The perception that online is cheaper.

And then, finally, our worthy challenge was defined as:

- Consumers are choosing convenience over experience.

Eureka! We had it. The key to the way you define the worthy challenge is to be accurate *and* to define it in a way that you can solve it. A local bookstore can't influence overall consumer purchasing behaviour, but they can address the experience they provide in their stores.

The next step was to decide on the Governing Approach. As you can see, how we defined the worthy challenge totally determined the Governing Approach we chose. If we'd defined the challenge as 'local bookstores aren't as convenient as online purchasing', then our Governing Approach would have focused on convenience. However, because we defined the worthy challenge as 'consumers are choosing convenience over experience', our Governing Approach became: Provide a breathtaking experience that outweighs convenience.

The bookstore owners looked excited. At last they had something they could do about a problem that seemed completely out of their control. The next step was to determine the action steps. The business owners launched into ideas, but at this point I pumped the brakes and asked, 'Has anyone asked the customer what breathtaking means to them?' No one had, so the next step for them was to go and talk to their customers and let *them* tell them what breathtaking meant so that appropriate action steps could be determined.

As you can see, this process is incredibly powerful. It has given small bookstore owners a way to compete effectively against Amazon and its massive resources, when before they felt helpless. That's the power of Planning for Results; it in itself becomes a major competitive advantage for your business.

HOW DOES A CRISIS CHANGE YOUR PLAN?

A crisis will sometimes call for a change of plan. The great thing about a crisis is that it presents an opportunity to suspend the old rules and create new ways of thinking and progressing.

The biggest mistake business owners make in a crisis is being content with returning to the status quo, thereby losing the opportunity to make progress.

The approach to a crisis is the same as the approach to Planning for Results: it starts with identifying the worthy challenge, then building the plan to deal with it in the same way.

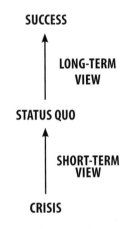

When I sustained that head injury in 2002, I had a choice to make: aim to return to the status quo, or aim to transcend the status quo. The status quo, my life as it was, was the reason I was in the mess I was in. So I realised that by just trying to get back to where I had been would mean I was destined to repeat my mistakes, and my life would quickly spiral downwards.

So I decided to transcend the status quo, to put aside the old rules I had for my life and the old beliefs I held about myself – to create a new reality, a new life. Everything good in my life has come from creating this new reality. Everything.

I needed to determine the actions I would take on a day-to-day basis to slowly recover, and to be able to pick myself up when I fell.

At the start I looked at my life in the short term. I was just trying to survive and make it through. But as my recovery progressed, I also needed to create a wider vision for who I needed to become, and how I wanted my life to look if I wanted to transcend my old status quo.

When you're in the thick of the battle, it's not the time to be thinking about your higher mission and where you want your company to be in five years' time – you need to stay alive.

To stay alive, you need to focus on the short term: actions to take now that will get you out of the crisis.

And as you exit the crisis, you need to turn your focus to the longer term, because that's what will capitalise on the crisis, and that's what will create progress and, potentially, a long-term advantage.

Being aware of when you need to focus on the here and now and when you need to take a long-term approach is critical to both surviving and thriving in business.

MAKING IT REAL

Creating a plan with focused strategic priorities and tactical activities is not the ultimate goal of planning; the ultimate goal is to drive the results you want in your business.

To ensure that your plan is effective, it is critical that you do two things:

- First, it's important to gain agreement from your team on the worthy challenge. They need to be on board, as everything is affected by how you frame the plan and the priorities you choose to focus on. This is critical, because only by doing this will the team fully buy into the output of this process, namely the plan.
- Second, you must ensure that the company, the team, is prepared and willing to take action on the plan once it is adopted. This is where you have to consider the repercussions of any decisions

and make sure that the company is aligned to moving in the direction you need.

For example, say you decide to change your target customer and, as a result, you forecast a temporary drop in sales in order to achieve a longer-term rise. Then you need to consider the compensation structure for your sales team. You need to ensure that the compensation structure rewards the focus and behaviours you want, otherwise the sales team is likely to keep doing what rewards them and your outcome won't be achieved.

And remember, the goal here is not a cool plan, the goal is results. Effective planning isn't finished until you execute the plan and put runs on the board. Many business owners fail on the execution front, so pay close attention to the following chapter, which provides a simple and effective framework to execute the plan you have created.

SUMMARY

Business planning can be a big, unwieldy beast, or it can be a tight, systematic process that moves you towards your target.

By defining a worthy challenge effectively, you will be able to build your Governing Approach and therefore carry out the appropriate actions to move you towards success.

Remember, most business owners focus on what they want, not what they are being called for. This leads to the creation of ineffective plans. By mastering this simple and effective planning method you can get off the scenic route and on the fast track heading straight to your destination.

You'll have a massive advantage over your competition.

That's just unfair.

That's winning the Unfair Fight.

ROUND 10

Execution

'If you have good game, your game is going to say that — you don't have to say it. Let your game be your promotion and your marketing tool.'

— MICHAEL JORDAN

There is a massive difference between having 'a good game' and having 'good game'.

In business, the difference between having a good game and having good game is execution, and the outcome of good game is sustained success.

Execution is the difference between a flash-in-the-pan win and a great business that consistently wins.

Most business owners are focusing on right now, on having a good game, but if you focus on developing good game, through exceptional execution, then you will win not only now, but also in the future.

Execution is the link that bridges the gap between what you want to achieve and what your business ultimately delivers.

Become an expert at execution and you'll be like Michael Jordan playing against a 10-year-old.

And that's just not fair.

WHOSE JOB IS EXECUTION?

As a young entrepreneur I thought my job was the vision, the growth, the future of my company. I thought execution was below me, that I could delegate that to someone else.

How wrong I was.

The leader sets the culture, and to have an organisation that is effective at getting things done, it is essential to have execution at the core of the culture.

If the leader isn't focused on execution, they can't expect the organisation to be focused on it.

When I palmed off execution to others in my business, I found that our great ideas started off well, but a year later I'd be asking what had happened to them. No one would know. The problem was that I hadn't placed enough importance on execution and, as a result, a lot of great ideas came to nothing.

How many great ideas have you taken action on only for things to fizzle out? How much has that cost you? Or, more accurately, how much has slipshod execution cost you?

Because execution is the bridge between what you want to achieve and what you actually achieve, it is a major responsibility of the business leader. Execution is not something to abdicate.

THE NINE CORE BEHAVIOURS OF EFFECTIVE EXECUTION

Execution is the discipline of exposing reality and acting on it. Because execution starts with the leader, they have to embody some key behaviours. These behaviours are what separate the leaders with all the good ideas and no runs on the board from the leaders who are able to take a vision and turn it into reality.

From personal experience I know that these behaviours can be learnt. Structure is the price the entrepreneur must pay for success, and these behaviours are the backbone of an effective structure.

The nine core behaviours are:

1. Being realistic

If your garden is overgrown with weeds, then no amount of covering your eyes and saying, 'There are no weeds, there are no weeds, there are no weeds,' is going to change the fact that your garden is a mess.

Execution must start with realism, because it is about getting from where you are now to where you want to go. As you've probably guessed by now, to make execution effective, you have to be clear on where you are now.

Many people don't like to face reality because it can be uncomfortable, so they hide their mistakes and skirt around the issues.

The leader must insist on realism and must be realistic themselves. A leader must be courageous enough to face up to the unpleasant facts that exist in any business, because only then can they ensure that the plan moves the business from where it really is to where they really want it to be.

Be realistic about both the strengths and the weaknesses in your business. Most business owners are great at knowing the strengths, and great business owners are also great at knowing the weaknesses.

Realism also requires an intellectual approach, because you need to discover the problem and not just the symptom that presents. A business owner might exclaim, 'I am being real!' when they talk about dropping sales, but the reality is that dropping sales are only a symptom of the fact that the owner hasn't been 100 per cent engaged with the business. Until they get real, nothing can be done.

Only when you get real can you effectively solve the problems that stand between you and your goals.

2. Being knowledgeable

To be successful in business, you must be fully engaged in your business. This doesn't mean that you are doing everything, but it does mean that you are across everything important in some way.

It's about living your business.

Businesses that don't do execution well usually have leaders who are far removed from the day-to-day realities. The information they get is filtered via multiple parties, many of whom don't want to upset the boss. The information these leaders have to work with is inaccurate at best, and a complete fabrication at worst. It's akin to running your business through Chinese whispers.

Good leaders want to know both what's going well and what's not going well. They want to know the intricacies and the challenges their front-line staff face, and they are happy to roll up their sleeves and get stuck in when they need to.

Walk the floor, talk to your people, speak with your customers, and be inquisitive. To be effective at execution you need to become a detective and you need to know your business like a surgeon knows the inside of a body.

3. Knowing your people

Leverage can be achieved through many aspects of your business, and the most important one is your people.

People are required to execute a plan, so the plan must play to their strengths and mitigate for their weaknesses.

If you don't know your people well, their strengths, their weaknesses, their loves, their hates, their aspirations, their fears, their stressors, their motivators – everything about them – then it's hard to know what they are capable of and how they will be able to contribute to execution.

Great leaders develop personal connections with their people, they engage with their people, and as a result they get buy-in from them. A study by PricewaterhouseCoopers found that 75 per cent of change initiatives fail because of failure to engage the people.

Change is a cornerstone of execution, so great leaders understand that they must know their people and engage with them if they want to effectively get to where they want to go.

4. Setting clear targets

Staff will look where the leader looks. If a leader is not clear about where they want to go, if they don't have a clear vision and clear goals, then the team will be confused and will likely resemble a room full of sheep running in different directions.

When a leader has a clear vision and sets clear goals for his company, the team is more likely to resemble a flock of migrating birds, flying in unison, making constant progress towards their ultimate destination.

One important thing to note is that too many goals can also cause confusion. Humans can only focus on a handful of things at one time, so to better harness the power of the organisation, it's best to have three or four main goals.

Effective target-setting must be centralised, as that's the best way to ensure that goals are prioritised. When a business owner isn't fully checked in and has decentralised setting goals and strategy, the result can be too many competing goals, with everyone having different ideas. The outcome of effective goal-setting is focused goals, not simple goals.

> *'Perfection is achieved not when there is nothing left to add, but when there is nothing left to take away.'*
> — ANTOINE DE SAINT-EXUPÉRY

5. Prioritising

In any business there is competition for resources: time, money, people, and so on.

One of the most important functions of the business leader is resource allocation. This means choosing the highest-value activities for the business and focusing resources on those activities.

Without carefully thought-out prioritisation, resources will be spread thinly and nothing great will be achieved. It is also likely that resources will be wasted as people in the business feud for the scraps so that they can progress their own agendas.

Take time to think about what is of truly high value to your organisation, then peel back the unimportant layers, the meaningless meetings, the activities that make you busy but not productive, until you are left with the highest-value activities that move you towards your goals. Focus your resources there.

6. Following up and following through

As I mentioned, early on in my business career we came up with some great ideas, only for me to find many had died within a year. Focused goals mean nothing if people don't take them seriously, and the only way they will take them seriously is if they know you are going to follow up on them.

Failure to follow through is one of the biggest causes of failure to execute in businesses, and it is therefore one of the biggest causes of business failure.

Even average ideas that are well followed up and well followed through can deliver great results, but great ideas with poor follow-up and poor follow-through will fail every time.

When setting goals, be sure to create milestones and checkpoints, places where your team knows its work will be scrutinised. Then, without fail, make sure you follow up. It's as simple as that.

7. Measuring and rewarding the right behaviours

There are a million and one things your staff can do that won't move them in the direction you want, and there is a small number of things that will move them in the right direction.

Finding behaviours that produce the results you want, then measuring, reporting on and rewarding those is vital to effective execution.

Because, really, that's all effective execution is – ensuring that the right behaviours are done consistently to produce the results you want.

Reward the people who produce great results well, and make no apologies for not rewarding the people who don't. This is key to creating a high-performance culture that encourages excellence.

If people don't like this system, you don't want them, because the ones who do like it are the ones who add real value to your business.

8. Expanding your team's capabilities

For the business owner, execution requires having great lieutenants, great managers. To ensure consistent execution, it's important to have capable people in leadership positions, so it doesn't just all fall on you. Often tomorrow's best leaders come from the next generation within your business. One of the most important things you can do as a business leader is to expand your team's capabilities, to pass on your knowledge, so that they can continue to grow and are ready to step up when the time comes.

When you're under the pump it's very easy to give orders, and many business owners are under the pump all the time. But taking orders disempowers people and shrinks their ability to make good decisions. Coaching is educating people to make better decisions and, by doing this, you empower them to make better decisions by themselves.

At times, this method might feel like two steps forward and one step back, but it is essential to creating an empowered team.

Observe your people in action and provide specific coaching on what they can do better, on how they can improve, and on how you would make a decision in their situation.

Just-in-time coaching is crucial to creating a high-performance organisation that thrives. Just-in-time coaching is providing coaching as issues arise so it's relevant and fresh. It's one of the best ways

I know to help people to consistently expand their capabilities, and also a great way to deal with problems when they are manageable, rather than waiting until they are at crisis point – kill the monster while it's small.

Good leaders will ensure that they have someone whom they are grooming and coaching to step into their job. An insecure leader will protect their role so that only he can do it, but he won't be very effective and he is unlikely to make great progress. Make sure that you, and all your key people, know who their next-in-line is and make sure that she is coached on all the things she will need to know should she have to step into the role urgently.

9. Self-awareness

Know thyself. This is the maxim of anyone who wants to be exceptional in anything, including business.

To be effective at execution you must know yourself, all of yourself, so that you can play to your strengths, mitigate for your weaknesses, be honest with yourself and others, and deal with business and operational realities in an upfront way.

People are great at detecting incongruence, so the statement 'Fake it until you make it' isn't a great one if you want to get the best out of people – and you need to get the best out of people if you want to execute effectively.

Self-awareness comes from self-exploration and a commitment to bettering yourself, and the result is self-mastery. These types of leaders earn the trust and respect of their people, and the inner confidence that comes with living like this can inspire people to achieve great things. You will have gained a lot of self-awareness when you went through Part 1 of *Winning the Unfair Fight*.

Great leaders who are self-aware will hold themselves to high ethical and moral standards; they will do the right thing, and this will give them the strength and courage to do what needs to be done in the toughest of times. This is critical to execution.

Self-aware leaders also have the courage to hire people different from them and to deal with poor performers swiftly. Without this, execution is compromised.

Self-aware leaders are also humble enough to know that they aren't the 'be all and end all', that they are flawed, and that there are people who are much better than them at certain things. Because of this, they can gain maximum leverage and empower people to be their best.

Self-mastery is the goal of great leaders, and it's critical to execution.

As you can see, these nine behaviours are not necessarily innate, but they are all inherently learnable. Any business owner can decide to master these nine behaviours and, in doing so, will place themselves and their business at a massive advantage.

CREATING AN EXECUTION PLAN

In what I consider to be one of the definitive books on the subject, *Execution: The Discipline of Getting Things Done*, authors Larry Bossidy and Ram Charan make the powerful distinction that execution is the discipline that links the three core processes of a business: people, strategy and operations. I highly recommend that you continue to read this book if you want more detail about effective execution.

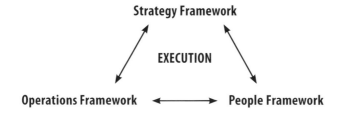

Execution plans can be complicated, but in my experience, complicated plans often don't work. What follows is the focused way to create an execution plan that both works and is able to be implemented by most people.

In Round 9 you learnt how to create effective strategies and tactics. This section takes it deeper by breaking down tactics into three frameworks: Strategy, People and Operations.

These sections are to be used in conjunction with Round 9.

1. THE STRATEGY FRAMEWORK
Linking people and operations

In Round 9 you learnt how to create an effective strategy – essentially, the top priorities that drive the direction of your business.

The Strategy Framework tells you how to create strategy and then how to link your People Framework with your Operations Framework. The Strategy Framework directs the action steps to achieve strategic priorities.

It starts with identifying goals, then defining the key issues behind those goals. It must take into account the market environment in which your business is operating, and it must define your competitive advantages and your 'moat'. Assumptions need to be identified and questioned, and alternatives must be considered.

It is imperative that you consider whether your business is actually capable of executing the plan. You must look at your organisational capabilities and your people: do you have the right people in place to achieve what you need to achieve? Is the plan flexible, or is it too rigid to adapt to a change in the environment?

When considering your plan, it is important to consider whether you have taken into account both shorter- and longer-term priorities. The businesses that thrive are the ones that keep an eye both on the present and on the future.

2. THE PEOPLE FRAMEWORK
Linking strategy and operations

People run your business, so this framework is essential. Having quality people to make sound judgements and take effective actions is at the heart of quality execution.

The People Framework must:

1. *Link people to strategic milestones and the Operations Framework*

You need to be very clear on the strategic objectives of the company and create milestones to move towards those objectives. You then use Critical Drivers to determine what needs to be done to achieve those milestones, and direct people to take those actions.

2. *Effectively evaluate and develop people*

Like anything in your business, you must have an accurate picture of your people. This needs to happen in an informal way through conversation and interaction, and also at set times when people receive their formal evaluations. A good leader will not have any surprises at evaluation time, because any issues will have been identified and worked through as they came up.

When you have a clear insight into your people, you can develop their talents and deploy them effectively, and you can up-skill in areas that need it. You can also remove the low performers who you can't bring up to scratch.

3. *Identify and develop leadership talent and ensure a solid leadership pipeline*

You can't expect your leaders of today to be your leaders of tomorrow. Things change for them personally, and the needs of your business also change. What works now may not work in the future.

It's imperative that you identify tomorrow's leaders and that you nurture them. Determine what skills and traits are important in your leaders, rate your future leaders against these, then develop plans to improve them. Some skills you might consider are: business acumen, customer insight, strategic insight, vision and purpose, culture, action, commitment, determination, teamwork, innovation, coaching, staffing and performance.

Download the Leadership Assessment tool to kick-start this process for you by registering at www.samhazledine.com.

When you effectively link your people to strategy and operations, they know what to do and how to do it. By evaluating and developing your team, you build a solid leadership pipeline. Now you have the foundations in place for excellent execution.

3. THE OPERATIONS FRAMEWORK
Linking strategy with people

The Operations Framework is the part of the plan that ties people to strategy. It is a guide to show people what to do.

This must be realistic. The process is not just making up a budget and saying, 'Go do it.' It must take into account the business's longer-term goals and break them into shorter-term targets.

It is crucial that the Operations Framework doesn't just look back to the previous financial year and add 10 per cent. It looks forward and maps out the 'how' for your people to achieve the strategic priorities you have identified.

Budgets are a core part of the Operations Framework and must be created using a process of robust dialogue where assumptions are questioned and people have a chance to have their say.

Building the Operations Framework requires three things:

1. Targets

Get clear on your targets: revenue, margins, gross profits, expenses, net profit, cash flow and market share. There will also be specific targets unique to your business. By getting very clear on these, you provide a measure by which to gauge your business's progress.

These targets need to take into account both the economic and market environment, and also your business and business units. Bossidy and Charan call this focus both on the market and on your business 'outside in' and 'top down'.

2. Action plans

Once you are clear on your short- and longer-term targets, you can determine exactly what needs to happen to achieve them.

Document an action plan for your business, and any individual business units, and break it down further to action plans for individuals.

Action plans should include the Critical Drivers of success.

3. Engagement and agreement

Remember that 75 per cent of change initiatives fail because the team is not engaged. Involve the team throughout the process so that by the time the Operations Framework is complete, they feel 'We did that.' Then you are more likely to have their buy-in.

The Strategy Framework is like the destination, the Operations Framework is like the car and the map to get there, and the People Framework is like the driver. You need all three working together well to ensure excellence of execution and to make sure that you reach your destination.

SUMMARY

Execution is critical for getting you from where you are to where you want to go, for taking an idea and making it real.

Many business owners are not good at execution.

An average plan executed well will deliver results; a great plan poorly executed won't. And a great plan executed well will knock the ball out of the park.

This chapter has given you three simple and effective frameworks – Strategy, People and Operations – to ensure that you become who you need to be and do what you need to do to execute exceptionally well. The rest of the book has given you an effective framework to ensure that you also have an exceptional plan.

An exceptional plan combined with exceptional execution means you will be lethal.

And that's just not fair on the competition.

That's winning the Unfair Fight.

PART 3

The Knockout

You can certainly be a very successful boxer by winning on points.

Part 2 gave you everything you need to win on points.

But is that really what great boxers want? Or are they looking for the knockout punch?

Part 3 gives you my secret weapons to deliver the knockout punch. Rounds 11 and 12 contain the 'secret sauce' that will make you unstoppable.

Master these final rounds and massive success will be yours.

ROUND 11

Stacking Your Corner

'The quality of your life is a direct reflection of the expectations of your peer group.'

I can clearly remember when I heard Anthony Robbins say this, because it turned my life in a new direction.

If you were going into a fight, would you want Muhammad Ali in your corner, or your alcoholic uncle?

The answer is obvious.

It doesn't matter how committed you are or how much desire you have, if you are dragged down by the people you have in your corner, then you're penalising yourself from the start.

And the reality is that most people in business are entering the ring with their metaphorical bum uncle, so they're getting slaughtered.

When you have the equivalent of Muhammad Ali in your corner, you give yourself an unfair advantage.

WHY DO YOU NEED TO STACK YOUR CORNER?
The fast track
There are two ways to learn:
1. The 'learn as you go' method, where you make your own mistakes and reinvent the wheel to grind out slow and laborious progress.

2. The fast track, where you learn from others and refine tested ideas to make fast and effective progress.

All the very successful people in business I know tend towards using the fast track, and being a bit stubborn, we also slip back to using the first method, get slapped, and are reminded why we use the second method!

If something has been done well before, the smart thing to do is to learn from that, then aim to improve upon it. By trying to reinvent the wheel you place yourself at a massive disadvantage, as you are starting well behind the pack.

When you become successful you will have learnt this, and you will learn this if you want to become successful.

The question is:

How expensive do you need to make the lesson?

When I started MedRecruit, I thought I was a wonder kid and could do anything better than anyone else. I decided there was no IT platform good enough for my business, so I built one from scratch. I gave away 20 per cent of my company in equity, as well as half a million dollars, and five years later I bought back the 20 per cent for a huge amount of money and threw out the system we'd built. Then I spent $150000 on an off-the-shelf product that we customised to do exactly what we wanted.

Lesson learnt.

There are people much better at many things than me and I'm now happy to admit that and to learn from them.

So, the first reason to stack your corner is to ensure that you are taking the fast track to success, which isn't just a fast way to disaster.

That's why you're reading this book. You are looking for the fast track, and that's smart.

Be a small fish

As I have noted, Anthony Robbins said, 'The quality of your life is a direct reflection of the expectations of your peer group.'

As human beings, most of us care to some extent about what people think of us. At some level we want to fit in and connect with those closest to us.

As a result we will adjust our expectations of ourselves to meet the expectations of those closest to us, and by doing this we adjust our personal standards, and therefore the results we get.

Dr David McClelland of Harvard University conducted research into high achievers and the factors that caused people to achieve highly, or not. After 25 years of research he concluded that the people with whom you associate yourself habitually can determine as much as 95 per cent of your success or failure in life. He calls the group of people you often associate with a 'reference group', and the choice of a negative reference group was in itself enough to condemn a person to failure and underachievement in life.

Dr McClelland's discovery provides evidence that your peer group is more important in determining your success or failure than any other single factor. Take heed.

While it might feel comfortable, being the big fish in a small pond is the surest way to place limits on your success. To grow – both yourself and your business – it's much better to be the smallest fish in a really big pond.

While this might feel uncomfortable, being surrounded by people who are playing at a higher level than you will mean that growth will only happen once you move through that discomfort and you start to elevate your own game.

If you are overweight and you want to get fit, then it's a bad idea to team up with an overweight friend who also wants to get fit. That will be an attractive option because it will feel safe, but it won't be an *effective* option. Your current fitness is a result of your past standards for eating and exercise, as is your overweight friend's. Putting two people together with low standards for eating and exercise is less likely to lead to great fitness and more likely to lead to watching TV and eating pizza on the couch together.

If you really want to get fit, go where the fit people are, those who hold themselves to the standard you want to achieve. Initially you'll feel uncomfortable because their high standards will highlight your low standards, but this will make you raise yours, and that is what will lead to positive change.

Similarly, in business, if you want to be successful, don't surround yourself with the majority of struggling business owners. All that will do is give you people to complain with and keep you playing small. Surround yourself with really successful businesspeople making a lot more money than you and you will be forced to raise your standards just to stay in that peer group – the results will follow.

When you surround yourself with this successful peer group, it's important to do so with a feeling of positive expectancy. Go into this group knowing that if they can do it, so can you. Actually expect yourself to achieve at their level. Don't feel bad about yourself because you aren't already at their level. Don't make where you are right now wrong. If you go into this group and feel unworthy or belittled, then the group can have the opposite effect, as it can cause people to give up, and that's certainly not the point of this.

So the second main reason to ensure that you stack your corner is to raise your standards. Then you raise the level of the game you are playing, and the results you get.

In addition, being around people who are playing at a higher level than you allows you to expand your belief that you can also play at a higher level – it gives you something to reference yourself against.

HOW TO STACK YOUR CORNER
Education

People are always asking me how to get great mentors and peer groups. You'll see the influence of many great people in my life and in this book, but how did I get to know people like Anthony Robbins and Keith Cunningham? The reality is that I didn't get to know people like this personally in the beginning. The first thing I did was commit to my personal education and personal growth.

A commitment to your own personal education is critical to stacking your corner, because you can gain access to the greatest minds and thinkers in history. And that can be as simple as reading a book or listening to an audio programme.

By exposing yourself to the great thinkers you are able to see *how* they think, and you can start to think like they do and act like they do. You can get to know them through their work.

A great way to actively educate yourself is to make a list of the key skills you need to learn, then to find the best resources on those subjects. Read the books, listen to the audio programmes, attend the seminars ... whatever it takes. Make sure you absorb what you need to learn.

When I started MedRecruit, I realised that to earn more I needed to learn more, and as a result I've invested over a quarter of a million dollars in my own education. You don't need to invest that much: I did because I was so driven to learn from the best, and because I knew that any money invested in effective education would come back to me tenfold. This book is the distillation of all that learning – I should raise the price!

Another approach you can take is to make a list of the people who have best mastered the skills you want and read their biographies for insight into not just what these people did, but how they thought. One of the books that most shaped how I do business was not a how-to business book, but the biography of Steve Jobs by Walter Isaacson. This book gave me an insight into how Steve Jobs thought, and the way that played out in his business, so I was able to learn both from his successes and his mistakes.

Apple is a fantastic example of how thinking like David can lead to great success. They started as the perceived underdog and, by using unconventional tactics, grew into the biggest company in the world.

Your personal education must become a top priority for you. It's a marathon, not a sprint, so set aside time every week (or even better, every day) to expose yourself to something that will help you learn and grow.

*Check out www.samhazledine.com
for some resources to get you started.*

Modelling

Modelling is a great way to accelerate your results.

Most people think modelling is simply looking at what someone did, then replicating that. But this mistaken belief means that most people fail to effectively model others.

You can't look at an action in isolation without considering the context that action was taken in.

To effectively model someone, you have to look at these three things:

1. What they did and the external environment they did it in.

2. The decisions that led to their actions.
3. Their internal environment – belief systems.

Picking people to model

I personally believe that the most appropriate model is a person who has actually achieved the results that you want to achieve. I would never look to model a person who hasn't achieved what they're teaching in the real world. I wouldn't look to model a 'business guru' whose only business success is in teaching people what to do.

Look for people with real-world success in business, health, fitness, relationships ... whatever it is you want to be successful in. Then read their books, read their biographies, study their lives and the decisions they made, and determine the next three things:

1. The actions they took and the external environment they did it in

The first thing to look at is what they did, but you can't look at this without considering at the same time the environment they did it in.

The right thing at the wrong time is the wrong thing.

So look at how the person considered the external environment and then took action to benefit from that.

Some questions that can guide you are:

- What did they do?
- How did they do it?
- What preparations did they undertake?
- What kind of economic environment did they do it in?
- What kind of social environment did they do it in?

2. The decisions that led to their actions

The next thing to do, which is equally important, is to look at the decisions they made that led to their actions, the choices they made about what actions not to take, and their decision-making process.

This is necessary because your environment is unlikely to be exactly the same as theirs. Effective modelling is being able to start to think like that person and to be able to make decisions like them.

Ultimately you should ask yourself: 'What decision would this person make in this situation?' When you are clear on the things they considered and the process they used to decide, you give yourself the best chance of making a decision like they would make.

Some questions that can guide you are:

- What problems were they solving?
- Why did they do what they did?
- Why did they choose not to do something?
- What factors did they consider in making their decisions?
- Were they looking to capitalise on an opportunity or avoid a disaster?

3. Their internal environment – belief systems

When you start to understand how someone made a decision, you will begin to get an insight into their belief systems.

To effectively model someone you must understand the belief structure that supported the decision and led to action.

If someone made a decision with the belief 'This is life or death,' it is very different from someone who made the decision with the belief 'This is going to be fun.'

Equally, a lot of us believe that really successful people think that 'big is better'. But in my experience, this belief can often hinder growth.

'Better is better' is a very different belief that will lead to very different decisions and very different actions and therefore very different results.

Often people won't share their beliefs, but a great way to find these out is to read their biographies and, through their stories and values, their beliefs will become evident.

Some questions that can guide you are:

- What did they believe was possible?
- What did they value?
- Who was most important to them?
- What was most important to them?
- Why did they see this as a must?
- What did they make non-negotiable?
- Who did they see as responsible for making this change?
- How much importance did they place on the change?
- What were they prepared to give up to achieve their goal?

When done effectively, modelling is a powerful way to both accelerate your progress and massively increase your chances of success.

Peer group

Your peer group has a huge impact on the level at which you choose to play.

I remember reading that many of the men who had held the world 100-metre running record had more than one older brother. This makes total sense, as from day one they had to run faster to keep up with their older brothers.

While they may not have been as fast at the time, the act of constantly striving meant that they created momentum and ended up faster, much faster.

In the same way it's important to surround yourself with people who are 'faster' than you. Allow yourself to feel uncomfortable, but then strive to get faster.

As Jim Rohn said, 'You are the average of the five people you spend the most time with.' This is true for income, health, relationships, happiness: all the important stuff.

The point is, we become the people we spend most of our time with.

So ask yourself: Who am I spending most of my time with? Do I want to be like them? Because whether you like it or not, you are becoming like them.

Consciously seek out the people you want to be like, go where they go, get to know them, make your peer group the people who hold themselves to a higher standard, and raise your standards.

If you look at your current peer group and realise that they aren't the people you need, then you have a decision to make. Are you prepared to sacrifice your future to save yourself the discomfort of changing peer groups, or is your future important enough for you to make an upgrade?

When you say 'Yes' to something, you say 'No' to something else. You need to be conscious of the fact that the peers you are saying 'Yes' to might be causing you to say 'No' to the future you most want.

This might require some courageous decisions; your future literally depends on this.

If you follow just one piece of advice in this book, make it this piece, because your peer group has the power to hold you where you are, to pull you back, or to lift you to new and greater heights.

Because it may be hard to find the exact peer group you need in the place where you live, you might want to look further afield. To get associated with some great businesspeople, I am part of a group of internationally successful businessmen that we call the Brotherhood. Some of these guys are achieving things I only ever dreamt of, but the fact that we talk monthly has raised the expectations I have of life, and of myself, because I don't feel comfortable playing small among this group. This raises the bar for what is now my new norm.

Mentors and coaches

We all have blind spots; none of us can see ourselves in action. Most of us are also tainted by not wanting to see our weaknesses.

All top performers have someone to help them improve. Even Michael Phelps, the greatest Olympian ever, had a coach, because he couldn't see himself swimming.

We all need someone to watch us from the outside, to see what we're doing well and to point out where we can improve. All top athletes have a coach, and all top businesspeople have either a coach or a mentor.

When seeking out a business coach or a mentor, it's important to look for three things:

1. They have got great results in business

Business success is very different from business theory. Most books about business are written by people who aren't in business, which is why the books aren't worth the paper they are printed on. Business is messy, and you need someone who's been in the trenches and knows what it's really like. Would you rather go to war after learning from a Navy SEAL or from a military academic?

2. They have a high level of insight

While business is messy, it's also an intellectual sport. A few people just get lucky in business, but most people create their own luck. You need someone who doesn't just think business is all done on gut instinct; you need someone who has a high level of insight they can apply across a range of different scenarios.

3. They are committed to, and excited about, learning

You want to learn from this person, so you want someone who loves learning and also loves teaching. In business, the height of the net is constantly changing; the shot that worked yesterday won't necessarily work today. People who love learning are constantly upgrading their knowledge and aren't stuck in the past or in one way of doing things.

A great mentor or coach can teach you what's worked for them, and they can also share how that may or may not work now.

The difference between a mentor and a coach is that a mentor is in business and a coach's business is their coaching. This is a very important distinction. Both mentors and coaches can offer you a huge amount, as long as they have been there and done it themselves. In my experience, many business coaches are failed businesspeople who have taken the easy option to teach what they can't do themselves – run a mile from these people. If you are getting a coach, find out what they've done themselves.

For coaching options, check out www.samhazledine.com.

Constant upgrading

Constant dissatisfaction with the status quo is the hallmark of a great leader.

A commitment to constant upgrading is essential for you to be the best you can be in business. Consistently upgrade yourself, your systems, your people, your point of difference in the market ... everything about you and your business.

Stacking your corner means that you expose yourself to ideas and people who are resonating at a higher frequency than you, and a commitment to constant upgrading means that you will take these ideas and these people and use them to become better yourself.

The average life cycle of an industry is 10 years, so it's no surprise that 96 per cent of businesses don't survive that long. Change is inevitable in business, but only the minority of business owners is committed to constant upgrading. These are the ones who survive the bad times and thrive in the good times.

If you want sustainable and long-term success in business, then constant upgrading is a must.

SUMMARY

In any fight, you want to give yourself the best chance of winning, and to do that you need to stack your corner.

Business is messy, it's roll-up-your-sleeves action, and without a strong corner you place yourself at a massive disadvantage.

A business is a reflection of its leader, so leaders must constantly upgrade both themselves and their business to create excellence.

To stack their corner, effective leaders will put themselves in situations where they aren't the biggest fish. They will seek out opportunities to be the smallest fish so that they feel compelled to upgrade their standards and to learn from people playing at a higher level.

Effective leaders will commit to ongoing education, to learning from the greats, so that they can take the fast track to success rather than making it all up themselves.

Great leaders will effectively model people who have achieved what they want to achieve, by learning how they made their decisions and what beliefs were driving them.

Most of your competition is comfortable with just maintaining the status quo, which is great for you, because the status quo of today is tomorrow's history lesson.

When you stack your corner, you are able to not only move with the changing conditions, but you become able to shape the status quo of tomorrow.

And that's just not fair on your competition, which is left in the past.

That's winning the Unfair Fight.

ROUND 12

The Power of Questions

I believe that in business, as in life, there are no complicated answers, there are only complicated questions.

Ask a better question and you'll get a better answer.

Get a better answer and you'll take better action.

Take better action and you'll create better results.

It all starts with the question you ask.

The majority of people don't realise that one of the most powerful tools they have available to them is the ability to ask focused questions.

We've been teaching this to our three-year-old daughter Zara. As with many three-year-olds, there was a lot of 'I can't do this' and 'I can't do that.' We taught her 'Ask a better question, get a better answer,' and we decided that instead of 'I can't ...', a better question would be 'How can I ...?' So now she has trained herself to ask 'How can I ...?' when she comes to a tricky situation, and she is able to find solutions.

And she's a three-year-old.

Questions direct our focus, which determines our experience and what we pay attention to, and therefore the meaning we give to situations. Questions are the ultimate force that controls our present and our future.

You need to know how to use questions effectively to harness their true power, and when you can do this, you give yourself an unfair advantage.

This chapter gives you the absolute knockout punch to accelerate your business success. What I will share changed my life as much as anything in this book. Trust me and read on ...

WHY ARE QUESTIONS CONTROLLING YOUR LIFE?

One of the first things I learnt from Anthony Robbins was 'energy flows where focus goes'. The most effective people are the most focused, because they are able to concentrate their energy like a laser. Most people's energy, and focus, is dissipated and is therefore largely ineffective.

Think about it in relation to your life.

When was a time when you were incredibly effective and achieved great things? Were you focused?

When was a time when you wanted something but seemed to spend all your time standing still? You were busy but not getting where you wanted to be. Were you focused, or not?

Questions are the way our brain determines what we are going to focus on.

In Round 1, Decide, I shared three questions that drive the decisions that shape your life:

1. What am I going to focus on?
2. What does it mean?
3. What am I going to do?

Whether consciously or subconsciously, you are asking these questions every moment of your life, and the answers are determining whether you are successful and fulfilled.

And it all begins with: 'What am I going to focus on?'

You are self-made. This is a lot easier to stomach when you're a self-made success, but it is equally true when you are a self-made failure.

Successful people focus on very different things from unsuccessful people. Whether they are doing it consciously or subconsciously, a successful person is spending the majority of his time focusing on things that move him forward, while an unsuccessful person is spending the majority of her time focusing on things that keep her where she is or pull her backwards.

What is important here is that a successful person is not spending 'all' his time focusing on things that move him forward, he is spending the majority of time.

A blind optimist spends all her time focusing on the future, a failure spends most of his time focusing on the past, and a successful person spends the majority of his time focusing on things that will move him forward, and some important time focusing on the problems of the present so that he can overcome them and move forward.

And this all started with the question: 'What am I going to focus on?'

Then it might have gone like this:

- What do I want?
- Why do I want it?
- What's currently in my way?
- What does it mean?
- What am I going to do to move myself from here to there?

Effective questions lead to effective answers, which lead to effective actions, which lead to better results.

Ask a better question and you'll get a better answer.

WHAT'S YOUR DRIVING QUESTION?

Anthony Robbins taught me that there is a question that drives each of us, a question that is so powerful that it is filtering our entire experience of life, and a question that we are unaware of most of the time.

That question is unique to each of us.

It is either shaping your life very positively or very negatively.

And it's shaping every aspect of your life: personal, relationships, business, health and fitness … everything.

You have been asking this question repeatedly as you read this book.

It's the question that we ask ourselves over and over throughout the day. It has been in your subconscious, but it's starting to move to your conscious awareness now.

I call this your Driving Question.

Examples of Driving Questions that negatively impact people are:

- What is wrong with me?
- Why do things never work out for me?
- What's wrong with this?
- Why do I always fail?
- Why won't this work?

This list goes on and on, and it's personal to each of us.

And while many people have a Driving Question that has a negative impact on them, some people have a question that has a very positive impact on them, such as:

- Possibility
- Care
- Transparency
- Excellence

No matter what your Driving Question is, your mind comes up with answers that support the nature of the question; that's just what your mind does – it can't help it. This is your self-talk and it has a massive impact on your level of success, your level of happiness and your confidence.

Every Driving Question comes to serve us, and it does at some level. My Driving Question used to be: 'What's wrong with this?' This question allowed me to find what was wrong so that I could fix it. I was on a constant mission to fix not only my business, but also myself.

This served me very well for a while because it meant I committed to constant and never-ending improvement in my life, which largely created who I am today.

However, focusing on what was wrong really started to suck the joy out of life, and it negatively affected my relationships because I was asking this question about everything and everyone.

Can you imagine asking 'What's wrong with this?' in relation to your loved one, and what that will do for that relationship? Trying to 'fix' someone you love is a bad strategy, trust me.

When I realised this, I took a close look at my life. I asked myself if I'd got all the good that I could out of that question. I realised that my commitment to constant and never-ending improvement was now so ingrained that it would always be a part of me. It was a huge blessing the question had bestowed upon me, and I realised that I didn't have to look for what was wrong to keep making things better.

So I made a conscious decision to change my Driving Question. I decided to go for my current question's antithesis: 'What's great about this?'

It was like a weight had lifted. I started to smile more, I enjoyed life more, and far from making me lazy, it made me hungrier to create even more greatness. It took my life to the next level.

Instead of just running a great business, I decided to write a great book about business. You can be the judge of the impact of changing my Driving Question.

Have you figured out what your Driving Question is yet? If you have, then great; if you haven't, then let's do it now.

Do you want to change it?

Let's go!

CHANGING YOUR DRIVING QUESTION

This is a deep process that requires your full attention and an investment of time. Do not do this until you can put yourself in an environment with no distractions for at least an hour. Total privacy is best (you'll see why) but not necessary (for the brave!). Relax and enjoy this because it has the ability to change your life for the better in a very powerful and profound way.

Go to www.samhazledine.com
to access the worksheet to support this process.

---

1. Determine your driving question

Do you know what your Driving Question is? Once you are aware that you have one, it usually comes to you pretty quickly. Don't filter it and, importantly, don't judge it. It is what it is and it came here to serve you.

If you're not sure what it is, here are some questions to help you figure it out:

- What is my life all about?
- What is life all about?
- What is important to me?
- What must I do to feel okay about myself?
- How do I feel about myself?

- How do I feel about life?
- Is life for me or against me?
- Do things work out for me or not?
- What do I focus on repeatedly?
- What am I saying to myself?

Take some time, sit with it. Your Driving Question will come to you. Write down your ideas.

Remember, don't judge it. It's okay, it got you to where you are now.

Now write it down on a piece of paper.

It's really important that you are very honest with yourself at this stage. If you filter and add a gloss to your Driving Question, then the rest of the process is much less effective.

When I first tried to diagnose my Driving Question, I added a filter. Instead of admitting my Driving Question was 'What's wrong with this?', I made it 'How can I make this better?' The difference is subtle but profound. While I was looking for what was wrong so that I could improve it, the true question was 'What's wrong with this?' By making it more palatable and pretending it was 'What can I improve?', I spent years trying to change it, to limited effect.

With further self-exploration I realised what my Driving Question really was and, as soon as I admitted this, I was able to make the change.

The truth will set you free.

Save yourself the years and get honest today.

2. Determine how it served you

Your Driving Question came to serve you, and it has. While you might not like some of the things it's costing you now, it's important to acknowledge it for the good it has done, because only then can you decide if its job is done.

Write down all the ways your question has served you. Give it the credit it deserves, be grateful for it. How has it shaped your life positively? How has it shaped your relationships positively? What has it done to help you? What behaviours or habits has it created in you that have a positive impact on your life?

Once you have completed that process, sit with it and be grateful, as this question has shaped you in wonderful ways. It is really important that you do this, because only then will you be truly free to let it go.

3. Determine what it is costing you

There is a cost to every Driving Question; some costs are large, some are inconsequential. It's now time for you to be brutally honest and write down what your Driving Question has cost you in the past, and is costing you right now.

How is your Driving Question negatively affecting your life? How is it negatively affecting your relationships? How is it hurting you? How does it make you feel about yourself?

Project yourself into the future and write down what it will cost you if you don't change your Driving Question. This is a really important step, because you will get an insight into how a lack of change will impact your life.

4. Determine if you need to make a change

Look at the ways your Driving Question has served you, and look at what it's costing you, and ask yourself: 'How could I get these benefits without the costs?'

Are some of the good habits so ingrained in you now that they are a part of you, with or without the Driving Question? I imagine that the fact that you are reading this means they probably are.

Is it time to let go and to create a new Driving Question that gives you all of the upside with none of the downside?

5. Picking your new driving question

Now it's time to have some fun. Brainstorm a number of questions that would give you all the upsides of your old question, with none of the downsides.

You might think of things that are the antithesis of your old Driving Question; this is what worked well for me.

Or you might think of something that completely transcends your old question. 'What's wrong with this?' might become 'Where's the gift in this?' Or it might become 'What's perfect about this moment?' Or even, 'How can I experience universal love even more in this moment?'

The key to a great Driving Question is that it:

- Focuses you in the present moment.
- Focuses you in a way that makes you feel great.
- Focuses you in a way that is important for you and aligns with your values.
- Focuses you in a way that has a positive impact on your life and the lives of others.

Sit with this, play with this, have fun with this.

This is not a step to rush. When you come up with ideas write them down, look at them, say them out loud.

Test each idea against the four criteria above.

When you have it you'll know it is right, because it will feel fantastic.

Congratulations, your life is about to change for the better.

6. Install your new Driving Question

You've been running your old Driving Question for a long time, so it's going to take a real commitment and process to install your new one.

Some of these steps might seem over the top but, trust me, they're not. You've been playing that old record for a long time, and you know how it is when you've got a song in your head and you can't get it out!

Think of 'It's a Small World' – if you've been to Disneyland, you'll understand!

1. Decide

First make the decision that you are committed to this. You are committed to do whatever it takes to install your new Driving Question. This is critical, because your old Driving Question will take any opportunity it can to stick around.

Write down your commitment and why you are committed to making this change. What has it cost you in the past? What will it cost you in the future not to change? What will you gain from making the change?

2. Scratch the old record

To stop a record playing, you can just take it off the record player, but to prevent it from ever being played again, you need to scratch it.

To 'scratch the record' of your old Driving Question, you need to interrupt it and confuse it.

Here's what to do (this is why you might want to be by yourself!):

- Say your old Driving Question.
- Say your old Driving Question while laughing at it. Do this for one full minute.
- Say your old Driving Question in a Mickey Mouse voice.
- Say your old Driving Question while spinning to the left.
- Say your old Driving Question while spinning to the right.
- Say your old Driving Question backwards.
- Do anything else wacky you can think of while saying your old Driving Question – your aim is to scramble it up any way you can.

Have fun – do this with a smile on your face. The aim is to get to the point where just hearing your old Driving Question sounds absolutely ridiculous.

When this happens, you are done with this stage.

3. Install your new Driving Question

Install: For 30 minutes to an hour you need to combine physical movement with saying your new Driving Question out loud. Go for a walk or a run and say it over and over. Say it with a smile on your face; enjoy it.

Embed: For the next 30 days, start your day by saying your new Driving Question out loud for at least five minutes. Remember the NASA study of astronauts that showed that for anything to become a new habit it needs to be done for 30 days with no break? This needs to be done every day for a minimum of 30 days. Do whatever it takes to remind yourself to do this each morning: put a note by your bed, put a reminder in your calendar, write it on the bathroom mirror … whatever it takes.

Ingrain: Make your new Driving Question part of your life. Write it down and put it in places where you will see it every day. Say it whenever you get a chance. Say it every day at least 24 times. Say it out loud, say it with a smile, say it in an empowered state.

Although this is a simple process, the challenge for you is to follow these steps and to have the self-discipline to install your new Driving Question, then to ingrain it and keep it alive every day.

Your old Driving Question might try to rear its head if you get in a low state. If you notice this happening, just focus on your new Driving Question and say it out loud, with energy.

When you take control of your new Driving Question and install it effectively, it's like strapping a supercharger to your life. You become the person you always knew you could be, and life becomes a lot more fun, too.

To access the full worksheet, Changing Your Driving Question, register at www.samhazledine.com.

WHAT IS YOUR BUSINESS'S DRIVING QUESTION?

You might be thinking: This is a business book, why is Sam going on about my Driving Question?

Well, that's a good thought and I'm glad you thought it!

Your business is a direct reflection of you and your psychology. It never ceases to amaze me how I can look at a business and instantly know a lot about the owner.

So if you don't like what your business is telling you about yourself, then the first thing to change is yourself. That means getting a Driving Question that serves you at the highest level.

After learning about my own Driving Question, I realised that a business can also have a Driving Question and that it can have a very profound impact on the success of that business.

A business is made up of many people with many unique Driving Questions. This means there is quite a different process to installing a Driving Question for your business.

1. Choose a great Driving Question

For a business, I don't waste time trying to determine what the Driving Question has been in the past. The business may or may not have had one and, regardless, it doesn't matter. What's important is what you choose as your Driving Question from this point on.

A business's Driving Question will direct the team's focus in a way that makes the business excellent in the present and moves it towards a compelling future.

The Driving Question will direct the behaviour of the team to be absolutely aligned with the culture; it's like their short cut to live the culture.

Here are some questions to help you determine it:

- What experience are you striving to create for your customers?
- What needs to happen to achieve this experience?
- How does the team need to behave?
- What does the team need to believe?
- Why is this important?
- What are our values?
- What is our culture?
- Where does our focus need to be to create the best experience we can for our customers?

Ask your team these questions and engage with them to determine the Driving Question that will serve your business at the highest level. Your team needs to be engaged, they need to be involved, because they need to take ownership of this question.

In MedRecruit, our culture is:

- possibility;
- care;
- transparency; and
- excellence.

While these values are succinct and easy to remember, we realised a question would help people focus on what they could do in the moment to live the culture and deliver at the highest level to our clients.

We came up with: *What more can I do?*

When the team asks themselves this, they are living the culture, they are going the extra mile for our clients, and they are helping each other out in any way that they can.

It's a simple question, and it's powerful.

2. Installing your business's Driving Question

Once you have determined what your Driving Question is, you need to install it across the business; that is, you have to install it in every member of your team.

If you have engaged the team to determine the Driving Question, this is going to be infinitely easier.

The first thing to do is to make the Driving Question part of your everyday language. Businesses run on rituals, so make it a daily task to ask each other the question.

Make the Driving Question visible and front of mind. Put it up around the business, get it on people's desks; wherever you look, it will be there.

Make it part of what you measure and report back on, and preferably what you reward on. Assess how well people are living the Driving Question and reward them accordingly.

The Driving Question for your business is one of the simplest ways I have found to ensure that everyone lives the culture and focuses in the best direction to create excellence.

Chances are none of your competition is doing this, so their focus is dissipated; trust me, it's rare.

Create your business's Driving Question, focus your entire team like a laser on what is important, and your business will flourish.

It will be like entering the ring with your competition blindfolded and punching in every direction. Then you line them up and knock them out with a single, focused punch.

And you won't even break a sweat.

PAUSE AND PONDER

Now that you understand that questions control your focus, and that by asking the right question you can focus your power much like a laser focuses the power of light, you'll want to focus that laser in the right direction and use its full potential.

Gloria Mark, a professor of informatics at the University of California who studies digital distraction, has shown that your average office worker switches activities every three minutes and five seconds. It then takes an average of 23 minutes and 15 seconds to get back to the original task, and 18 per cent of tasks never get returned to.

This not only results in stress and low productivity, but it also results in superficial thinking.

It means that all you ever do is scratch the surface of what you're capable of.

But that can be changed.

Because the majority of your competition is working with dissipated focus, you can use this as a massive advantage.

The great philosopher René Descartes was once taking time out from battle and said, 'Being away from the front and having no female companions to worry about or no war to fight, it occurred to me that I'd have time to think.' And he started to question everything more deeply, which eventually brought him to: 'I think, therefore I am,' which, he said, was the first thing we could really be certain of.

But it's almost certain that Descartes would not have come to one of the most profound distinctions in human history had he been busy checking emails and fielding interruptions.

You have to take time out of the hustle and bustle of everyday business, or the battle of business, to clear your head and really think. It's incredible what your brain will come up with when you give it the chance to operate at its best.

And all it takes is the discipline to do three things:

1. Define the objective

You can only focus effectively on one thing. So the first thing to do is to define what you are trying to achieve. Are you looking for a solution to a problem, or are you looking to diagnose the problem?

2. Focus your attention with a question

You know the drill by now: ask a better question and you'll get a better answer.

We think by answering the questions we ask ourselves. Is that right? I bet you just asked yourself that question. So the next step is to put up some Guiderails to focus your attention.

For example, if you're trying to diagnose the problem, you might simply ask: 'What's the problem?' Or you might take that in a different direction and ask: 'How did we get to this undesirable situation?' Or, 'What did I miss that led to this situation?'

If you're trying to come up with the solution to a problem, you might ask, 'How can we capitalise on this situation?' Or, 'How can we avoid this in the future?' Or even, 'How can we turn this into a competitive advantage?'

Craft your question so that the answer will deliver exactly what you need.

3. Do the time

You now know that it takes about 23 minutes to get yourself focused again after every interruption, so you need to ensure that the time you spend pondering your situation is uninterrupted. Do whatever it takes or don't waste your time.

Personally, I find that 30 minutes is a minimum period of time and, if I'm on a roll, that might extend to an hour. Very rarely do I get good ideas in less than half an hour, and very rarely am I able to stay focused beyond an hour.

Actually, using your brain is one of the most powerful things you can do to solve problems, to come up with differentiation strategies, to improve the service you offer . . . the list is limitless.

It takes self-discipline, which most people don't demonstrate, so if you do, you're giving yourself an unfair advantage over your competition.

SUMMARY

Most people never realise that the questions they ask themselves determine the answers they come up with, and the actions they take, and the results they achieve.

Most business owners never understand that their business is a reflection of their own personal psychology.

Simply by understanding this, you give yourself an unfair advantage. You take control of both yourself and your business and you focus your power in the direction you want.

You are now in a position to create your own Driving Question to supercharge your life.

You can create a Driving Question for your business so that your people know where to focus.

Your competition is caught up in distracted, superficial thinking, so by using questions effectively, it's like having Einstein up against a distracted five-year-old in an intelligence test.

And you can use your powerful brain as it was intended, by getting clear on what it needs to focus on, asking it a great question, and then doing the time to come up with superior answers and action steps.

And that's just not fair.

That's winning the Unfair Fight.

THE EXTRA ROUND

Impact

What's the best way to help poor people? Don't be one.

I believe one of the biggest contributions you can make in life is to create a successful business.

I believe that the amount you earn is largely a reflection of the value you are providing.

Businesses create jobs and take people out of poverty.

A successful business means that you are making a positive impact on the lives of a lot of people, because if you weren't, you wouldn't be a success.

A successful business means that you are employing people, giving them jobs, giving them income, supporting them and their families.

A successful business means that you are empowering your people, helping them to grow, to become better people, and then they go out and have a positive impact on other people in an ever-widening circle.

A successful business means that you are making profit and therefore paying taxes. The more profit you make, the more tax you pay, which helps the less fortunate.

With financial success your influence can reach much further than your physical presence. So, to have the biggest impact, the first thing you need to focus on as a business owner is creating an exceptional business.

And once you have a successful business, you have the luxury of thinking about contribution beyond that.

WHEN SHOULD I FOCUS ON CONTRIBUTION?

I've been asked, 'When is the best time for a business person to start focusing on contribution?'

My answer is always: 'Right now.'

But where that contribution happens is very different, and depends at what stage your business is.

In the early stages of business – Flirting, Infancy, Child, Young Adult – that contribution must be focused on your staff and your customers. If you spend too much energy on contribution beyond these two core groups, then you are likely to miss the opportunity to create a great business.

When you've created a sustainable, profitable business, a business in Optimal, then you have the opportunity to become a wider force for good. Now you can start looking beyond your staff and your customers to where else you can have an impact, if that's what you want to do.

People who create successful businesses are already having a wider positive impact, and many business owners find that when they get their business to Optimal, they feel the need to go even further. They want to have an impact on a cause of their choosing, an area where they see a real need and where they are passionate about making a difference.

Can you imagine what the world would be like if all successful business owners focused on having a positive impact, both locally and globally? How many of the world's problems would be solved?

THE HAZLEDINE FOUNDATION

After seven years of creating a successful profitable business, my wife Claire and I felt the need to broaden our impact. With success came everything we could want, but now we felt that it was time to help others to create success in their lives too.

We both feel passionate about supporting young people, because with their whole lives ahead of them, there is a great opportunity to have a real positive impact. We could see that while we're all created equal, we don't all get the same start in life, and we felt that there was the possibility to contribute, even in a small way, to the start that some young people were getting.

We set up the Hazledine Foundation on the premise that 'Everyone Matters'. We wanted to help young people believe in themselves and provide them with the tools and resources they need to be happy now and to create compelling futures, so that they can lead fulfilling and productive lives.

We started small by speaking to groups of young people in schools, and have evolved the foundation into programmes that have an ongoing impact on young people who need it most.

We are now partnering with people in South Sudan and funding missions to get children out of absolute hell, where they are being brutalised and forced to commit unbelievable atrocities. We are getting these children to orphanages where they are safe and have the opportunity to have a bright future – or even a future at all.

It's so easy to take all that we have for granted, but when you remember that most people in the world would trade their best day for your worst, doesn't it put your problems in perspective?

To broaden our contribution, for everyone who buys the book and then signs up for the resources that support *Winning the Unfair Fight* at www.samhazledine.com, I will donate the proceeds from your book to the Hazledine Foundation. This money will be used to continue our work in Africa, and together we will share the impact of the foundation.

Please visit the website, get the unpublished chapter, benefit from the free resources, and help us to impact the lives of young people who didn't get the same start we did.

SUMMARY

As a businessperson, the best way you can have a positive impact is to create an excellent business.

If you dissipate your focus before you've done this, then you risk limiting your success and, ultimately, the effect that you can have.

Successful businesspeople are usually generous people, because the more you give, the more you receive. Until you've created an Optimal business, I encourage you to focus your desire to contribute, to give, on your customers and your staff, because by doing that, you are creating leverage to build a great business.

When you have a great business with sustainable success, *then* you can look at opportunities to broaden your impact.

Mastering the Unfair Fight means focusing on excellence and creating a great business so that, ultimately, your ability to become a powerful force for good can be as big as you dream.

Making the Most of This Book

Success in anything, including business, cannot be achieved through learning and wishing.

Success is achieved through learning and doing.

Learning ensures that you are able to make the best decisions to take the best actions, which means you are more likely to achieve the best results and live the best life.

I am no different from most business owners. Like you, I've got a brain to think with and a body to act with.

Where I am different from most business owners is that I committed myself to creating a powerful psychology and I am relentless in taking action.

Did I always take the best possible actions? Heck, no. I've made a lot of mistakes, but I made them fast, I learnt, and I took action again. I did that enough to create the fastest-growing business-services business in the country.

Success doesn't mean never failing; it's about failing quickly and picking yourself up and acting again, until you get to your destination.

Remember the simple formula for success? If you fall over 1 000 times, then get up 1 001 times.

Successful people know that while failure is inevitable, defeat is optional.

This book contains the best of what I've learnt about running a successful business – who you need to be, and what you need to do. If I'd had this book when I started my business, there's no telling where I'd be now.

You have this book. I believe that you have the best of the best when it comes to educating yourself about what it takes to be successful in business. Remember, business success lies at the intersection of mindset and action.

But it will only be of use if you use it, if you take action.

To make taking action as easy as possible, so it's literally a 'fill in the blanks' exercise, I've created a lot of resources for you and loaded them onto www.samhazledine.com. You'll find templates, videos and other material to accelerate your success.

All you need to do is register, and you'll have access to these at no cost to you.

BE KIND TO YOURSELF, AND ...

You might have got this far and be thinking, *Great, I know exactly what I need to do*, or you might have got here and be overwhelmed and feeling like there's so much to do.

Here's the thing: one distinction, one single idea that you got from the book might change everything for you, or you might need a few. Regardless, it would pay for you to know that I certainly didn't do everything in this book when I started out in business. At the start I would say that what I mostly got right was the mindset stuff, and the rest I've learnt over the past seven years through education and my own mistakes.

Heck, I don't even get all of it right all of the time now, but I am striving to do better every day. Business is fluid, things change. You've got to be flexible and adaptable to be successful.

What I'm saying is that you don't need all of this in place to have a successful business – so don't be too hard on yourself.

But don't be too easy on yourself either.

You now know exactly what you need to do to create a really successful business, and that responsibility lies with you.

If you want to get six-pack abs, you can't get someone else to do your sit-ups for you.

If you want to create a successful business, no one else is going to do that for you. That is your job.

You are exactly where you need to be right now, and now is right on time. I encourage you to be grateful for where you are, wherever that is, and to become driven to create something better.

Don't beat yourself up if your business is in a mess and, equally, in a year's time don't let your results be a reflection of you not working hard enough.

Prioritise what you've learnt in this book, schedule time to put it into action, and get it done.

Don't strive for perfection, because that's impossible and you'll waste time. Strive for excellence and hold yourself to a new and higher standard.

If you're not sure what to act on first, make your best guess and get to it. I was once in a six-month coaching group and by the time some people had decided what to do first, I had acted on everything we had learnt. I'd found what worked for me, and I'd taken my business from being barely break-even to making over $60 000 in profit per month. And others were still talking about what to start with.

There is a time to talk, and a time to act. Don't confuse talking with acting; they aren't the same thing.

Trust your instincts on this: you are much more than you ever thought you were, so act definitively and start putting runs on the board.

The very fact that you've read this far puts you in the top 1 per cent who don't just see an opportunity and wish it would magically fall into their laps. You are in the minority who see an opportunity and see it through; apply that in your business and you will be unstoppable.

The reward you get will be a direct reflection of how much you put in. The 12 rounds have been laid out in a specific order for a reason. I encourage you to go through the steps in this book in order, mastering yourself first, then the core business skills you need, then the knockout punches that will propel you into the stratosphere.

THE THREE CORE DRIVERS OF SUCCESS
In addition, you can access the unpublished chapter that reveals the three core drivers of success by visiting www.samhazledine.com.

In this chapter I reveal how on a one-hour drive to present to a group of school kids I rewrote my entire talk on success to focus on the real drivers of success.

They deserved the truth, so I decided to give it to them.

You also deserve the truth. You can handle it.

This is the unfiltered version that people who wish for success but aren't committed don't like, because it's confronting. Those who are committed to success will love this chapter, as it gives them the exact framework to guarantee success in any endeavour.

Beyond the Fight

Congratulations on completing the 12 rounds of the Unfair Fight.

After the head injury I sustained in 2002, and the subsequent changes I made in my life, I realised that we are going to get to the end of our lives and ask ourselves three questions. The answers to these three questions will determine whether we have lived fulfilled lives:

- Did I live with purpose?
- Did I live with passion?
- Did I live with presence?

Living with purpose means that we have found the reason we have been put on this earth; we've found how we can make the biggest contribution, and we do it with excellence and act in a way that really matters.

Living with passion means that we have found that thing that makes our heart sing; we've found what we love and we combine that love with enthusiasm to really live every single day to the full and to make each day our masterpiece.

Living with presence is an outcome of living with purpose and passion; it's about living in the moment, knowing that there is no other moment that we can live in, and having the faith that in that moment we are doing exactly what we are meant to be doing and we are doing it with everything we have.

We need all three to lead a truly fulfilled life; we need to know why we're here, we need to be living each day to the full and we need to be living in the moment. These three things underpin everything.

My vision is that this book has helped you move towards being able to answer all these questions with a resounding 'YES!'

Creating a successful business that has a positive impact is an empowering way to live with purpose, passion and presence. It's a way to contribute on a scale that few people have the privilege of doing.

For me, finding that intersection between mindset and action, applying that in my business and life to improve my life and achieve my goals, and now sharing that with you to help you improve your life and achieve your goals, brings me purpose, passion and presence. So thank you.

I hope you have not only read the book, but that you've also taken action in every round; or if this is your first read-through, that you are going back to reread it and take action. I hope you've been to my website and downloaded the resources to take effective action. If you haven't, then I encourage you to do it now, because these resources are there to help you, to give you a short cut to success.

Remember, successful people do what unsuccessful people aren't prepared to do. I encourage you to be in the minority of people who not only learn, but who also act, relentlessly, energetically and passionately.

By now you will have realised that this book isn't about a fight at all – it's about creating excellence in your business and excellence in your life. You then actually remove yourself from the fight and put yourself in a league of your own.

The majority of businesses are thrashing it out with each other, and most of them are losing. Sometimes they are losing to big corporates, sometimes they are losing to other small businesses.

You have now seen that when you act unconventionally, when you do things a bit differently, when you don't buy into 'common knowledge', you can become like David and actually be the favourite against the lumbering Goliath.

When you choose mastery, when you choose excellence, when you live in the present with an eye to the future, you will create a great business with sustainable success.

When you focus on excellence, you'll go big. When you focus on getting big, you'll likely struggle; after all, pigs get fat, hogs get slaughtered.

Success is a process; it's a marathon, not a sprint. In fact, success in business is more like a decathlon because you have to get a lot of things working well together.

The most important thing you can do is decide to be successful, to cut off from all other options and to commit to your future, to the future that you define. You can then build a bulletproof psychology that will propel you in the direction you want.

Make the transition in your business from loving your product to loving your employees and customers, and become a leader who people respect and will follow. Build a team that is set up to succeed, that you are engaged with, and that allows you to use your time and energy to inspire.

Choose how you will differentiate your business – will you be creating a new category, positioning yourself as the authority in your category, or will you be the very best in your category? Then communicate that point of difference through effective marketing and close the business through New Sales, where you take the customer on a journey and meet their needs at the highest level, making them feel great along the way.

Become an expert in both planning and execution. Remember that execution is one of the most common causes of failure for entrepreneurs, so make this a priority. Structure is the price entrepreneurs must pay for success, so be prepared and pay the price, because the reward is worth it.

Immerse yourself in wisdom, in education, in a peer group that will lift you up, and find someone who will hold you accountable. Become a lifelong student and commit to stretching yourself every day. Your business is a reflection of you, so become more to earn more. And live more.

Direct your mind effectively with the power of questions. Harness your mind by taking time out to really think deeply and tap into the greatest resource you have available: you.

Success isn't complicated, it just requires taking good actions consistently. We are all creatures of habit, so make your habits ones that move you towards what's important.

Master the habits of winning the Unfair Fight simply by taking small actions every day and notice how your success compounds. You will get to a point where you take stock and realise how far you've come in a short period of time, just from doing the simple things consistently.

And at that point you'll realise the truth about winning the Unfair Fight – that by mastering yourself and your business, you transcend the fight through excellence.

And that's about as fair as it gets.

SAM HAZLEDINE

Suggested Reading

As well as suggested reading, each of these books has influenced *Winning the Unfair Fight* in a significant way.

Awaken the Giant Within: How to Take Immediate Control of Your Mental, Emotional, Physical and Financial Destiny! by Anthony Robbins, published by Simon & Schuster, 1991.

Tony is outstanding when it comes to creating a personal success psychology. This book will teach you some powerful strategies to help hone yours.

David and Goliath: Underdogs, Misfits and the Art of Battling Giants by Malcolm Gladwell, published by Little, Brown and Company, 2013.

This book provides in-depth proof of why David has the advantage over Goliath, and why, as the underdog, you actually have an unfair advantage.

Execution: The Discipline of Getting Things Done by Larry Bossidy and Ram Charan, published by Crown Business, 2002.

A detailed study of execution. This is a great read if you want more on this critical subject.

Good Strategy/Bad Strategy: The Difference and Why It Matters by Richard Rumelt, published by Crown Business, 2011.

Clears out the mumbo-jumbo underlying too many strategies and provides a clear way to create and implement a powerful action-orientated strategy for the real world.

Oh, the Places You'll Go! by Dr Seuss, published by Random House, 1990.

Read this to your kids, and the message is as relevant to you as it is to them; while life may be a 'great balancing act', 'there's fun to be done', so believe in yourself, know that you'll trip, but get back up and you'll guarantee success (98.75 per cent of the time!).

Steve Jobs by Walter Isaacson, published by Simon & Schuster, 2011.

Get an insight into the guy who created the biggest company in the world by acting like David, even when Apple became Goliath.

The Alchemist by Paulo Coelho, published in English by HarperCollins, 1993.

A wonderful parable about listening to your heart, about learning to read and act on the omens life puts along your path, and above all about following your dreams.

The Richest Man in Babylon by George Samuel Clason, published by Penguin Books, 1926.

You're going to make a lot of money by applying what you learn in *Winning the Unfair Fight*, and this parable will teach you the universal laws of money.

The Ultimate Blueprint for an Insanely Successful Business by Keith J. Cunningham, published by Keys to the Vault, 2011.

This is the best book I've read on making finances meaningful and understandable. You don't need to be an accountant to master your business finances, and after you read this book, you'll have a deeper financial understanding than most MBAs.

Think and Grow Rich by Napoleon Hill, published by The Ralston Society, 1937.

This is the book that started many great careers, including mine. It's not an easy read, but the principles are powerful and enduring.

Think Bigger: How to Raise Your Expectations and Achieve Everything by Michael Hill, published by Random House NZ, 2010.

A great read by a great Kiwi entrepreneur. This is a wonderful insight into what made Sir Michael successful.

References

'Branding 101: 12 Brand Archetypes' by Matt Schoenherr, http://marketingideas101.com/marketing-articles/branding-101-12-brand-archetypes/

Managing Corporate Lifecycles: How Organizations Grow, Age & Die (Kindle edition) by Dr Ichak Adizes, published by Adizes Institute Publications, 2012.

Nice Teams Finish Last: The Secret to Unleashing Your Team's Maximum Potential by Brian Cole Miller, published by AMACOM/American Management Association, 2010.

What to Do If Your Marketing Sucks by Richard Petrie, self-published e-book, 2013.

COMPETE HEAD TO HEAD AND YOU'RE DEAD
The statistics in the opening paragraph are from the Ministry of Economic Development and Statistics New Zealand respectively.

WHAT IS THE UNFAIR FIGHT WORTH TO YOU?
The information on average incomes is from the United States Government, usgovinfo.about.com/od/moneymatters/a/edandearnings.htm

Do you have any comments, suggestions or
feedback about this book or any other Zebra Press titles?
Contact us at **talkback@zebrapress.co.za**

*

Visit **www.randomstruik.co.za** and subscribe
to our newsletter for monthly updates and news

Other new business and personal finance titles by Penguin Random House

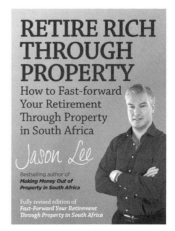

Also available as ebooks